UNRAVELING THE STORY OF
BLACK/AFRICAN HAIR

SAYE CARRIE

LAEL PUBLISHING

UNRAVELING THE STORY OF BLACK/AFRICAN HAIR
by Saye Carrie
Published by The Lael Agency
Winston Salem, North Carolina
www.LaelAgency.com

No part of this book may be used or reproduced in any form, stored in a retrieval system, or transmitted in any form by any means, electronic, photocopy, mechanical, recording or otherwise without written permission from the author. The only exception is for critical articles or reviews, in which brief excerpts may be used.

Paperback ISBN - 978-1-95-443300-7

Author's Photos: Jonathan Cooper/Coopernicus Photography

Author's Website: SayeCarrie.com

Copyright © 2020 by Saye Carrie Leneus
All Rights Reserved

First Edition

Printed in the United States of America.

Acknowledgments

I have to start off by thanking the almighty God for showing me what my purpose is. I also give thanks to my African foremothers, who passed down the magnificence and importance of Black/African hair. I also want to thank my mother Ceanea and my sister Emmalyn "Trudy," as well as my grandmothers, aunts, cousins, and hair stylist for their roles in the care of my hair. To the ladies I reached out to about my book, and who were excited and eager to share their hair stories—Ebony, Erin and Briel, Oju, Jade, Jasmine D., Jessica, LaTonya, Mary, and T.D—thank you! Also, to the lovely individuals who allowed me to showcase their hair, thank you from the bottom of my heart. Lastly, I give my sincere gratitude to my husband Fedner and my son Fedale for supporting me in my journey as an author.

Contents

Note from Saye Carrie.. 9
Saye's Hairstory Part 1.. 11
Introduction.. 13
Chapter 1:
The Significance of Black/African Hair........................ 15
Mary's Hairstory
La Tonya's Hairstory
Chapter 2:
The Commodification of Black Hair............................. 51
Jasmine's Hairstory
TD's Hairstory
Chapter 3:
The Natural Hair Movement of the 21st Century......... 81
Jade's Hairstory
Ebony's Hairstory
Chapter 4:
Conflicting Sides of the Natural Hair Movement......... 111
Jessica's Hairstory
Oju's Hairstory
Chapter 5:
Inclusivity within the Natural Hair Movement............ 141
Erin and Briel's Hairstory

Chapter 6:
Discrimination Against Natural Hair.......................... 167
Chapter 7:
Saye's Hairstory Part II... 189
References... 225

Note from Saye Carrie

For many generations, hair has been pivotal for Black women and girls. While some may think along the lines of "it's just hair," Black women and girls know that there is a deep history to our hair, as well as deep trauma that has become attached to it. Due to the effects of chattel slavery and colonialism, it has been embedded in our perceptions that Eurocentric hair and beauty standards are the norm, and something we should aspire to. For generations, negative connotations have been placed on our hair, including descriptions such as "nappy," "ugly," "wooly," or "rough."

As time passes, though, we are starting to see and accept the beauty and distinctiveness of our hair. Though others may ask why hair is such a big deal for us, what they fail to realize is that the importance of our hair started with our African foremothers. Hair and hair styles were identifiers of social status and even ethnic groups. Although some of us were not born in Africa or else in a lineage whose people have been out of Africa for hundreds of years, the significance of hair remains planted in our genes.

So, to my sisters who may still be struggling with their hair, take heed because we have all been there. Take this journey with me to untangle the truth about our hair. As we work each section at a time, you will begin to see the cornerstone of our amazing hairstory.

Saye's Hairstory Pt. 1

It was around late spring-early summer of 2010 and I had had my last relaxer in April. During that time, my hair was styled in kinky twists and I wanted to start transitioning it. In the meantime, though, I was trying to figure out what to do with it. In my mind, I was debating: should I continue relaxing my hair or return natural? Over the past eleven years, pretty much anything to do with my hair had been a battle. I would see some progress at times, and then other times go through major setbacks.

In late 2009, though, I was determined to stop relaxing my hair and just do Dominican blow-outs. Obviously, though, I couldn't just let go of the straight look I had had for the past eleven years all at once. When I went to a salon, I told the hairstylist I wanted a blow-out; however, she contested that my hair needed to be relaxed. I had a lot of new growth and as I look back, I feel that the stylist didn't want to deal with the two textures: at the time, my roots were natural and the ends were permed. I also was hesitant about returning natural because I had not seen my natural hair since I was about nine years old. Also, it had been my mother, sister, grandmothers, aunts, and family friends who were the ones taking care of my natural hair. So this was something new for me.

After my hair was relaxed the first time, my mother

gave me the leeway to style and maintain it the way I wanted to. So, I knew that once I returned natural, I would have to relearn my hair and manage it differently than I had in years. I was nervous about handling my most-likely type 4 texture. From viewing baby and childhood pictures, I knew that my hair was kinky with a tighter curl pattern. So, through summer 2010, I started to do my research on Black/African natural hair. At that time there were many natural hair blogs and forums as well as the rise of natural hair influencers on YouTube. While watching ladies such as Maeling Murphy (Natural Chica), Harmony Knight (I love my Fro), Toni Daley, SimplYounique, and more who captured their natural hair journeys and reviewed helpful products, I stumbled across a video that was dedicated to natural hair, particularly type 4 hair like mine. As I watched, tears began rolling down my cheeks because I was blown away at how eccentric, beautiful, and healthy those ladies' hair was! That video captured ladies whose 'fros were so big they could reach the sky and other gems with low-cut styles that brought out the beauty of their facial structure. After I saw this video, I began to regret ever chemically straightening my hair and I was eager to work toward returning natural.

Introduction

This book will discuss the history of Black hair and how it has tended to represent a person's ascribed status. Throughout the history of the Black hair movement, there have been many historical figures who greatly represented Black hair. However, even though there are many influential people who embrace Black hair and those who have created hair products for it, there is also a deep-rooted history of natural Black hair being depicted negatively. The media plays a part in the misrepresentation of Black hair as well, and from there it permeates society and impacts Black women's perception of their own hair. Thus, even when Black women and girls view Black hair magazines or commercials of Black hair, they try to emulate the hairstyle or aim for a style that is supposedly "acceptable" to society. The history and media portrayal of Black hair have led to the Black hair care industry becoming a $500 billion business because the main goal is to achieve what is considered "Good Hair."

However, there have been changes in the Black hair movement, especially recently. Many more Black women and girls are once again going natural instead of using chemicals to alter the true texture of their hair, or even wearing hair extensions, weaves, or crochet that have a similar appearance to their own hair texture. Yet, things are not always ideal or completely accepting, even in this movement.

This book will further discuss some of the controversial sides of the natural hair community, such as "texturism," policing natural hair, and many forms of discrimination facing natural hair and those who wear it proudly. It will also focus on inclusivity, which has been a "feather fuffle" throughout the natural hair community. Throughout this journey, I will include ladies, from myself to others I have interviewed, telling their own histories – or "hairstories," as I call them here – with learning to love their Black hair.

Chapter 1

The Significance of Black/African Hair

All women can attest to the struggles and successes that come with managing their hair. Regardless of race, we all vacillate over how to wear it; decide or change our minds about what color it should be, and sometimes cringe at the thought of cutting it too short. According to the American Academy of Dermatology (AAD), we are all born with approximately 100,000 hair follicles on our scalps. However, when the study of hair is broken down to different hair textures, not all hair is created the same. Visually, Black/African hair is thicker,

UNRAVELING THE STORY OF BLACK/AFRICAN HAIR

curlier, and often frizzier as compared to Caucasian and Asian hair. Coming from a grooming perspective, Black hair is also more sensitive to excessive manipulation, and so requires a different set of styling techniques.

Over the past 40 years there has been an enormous growth in the popularity and variety of Afrocentric hair styles worldwide, as the abundance of specialized African American salons in even the United States alone can demonstrate (Sieber and Herreman 2000). In their book *Hair in African Art and Culture*, Roy Sieber and Frank Herreman explore the beauty and significance of African hairstyles through the exhibition of fine collections of artifacts and images displayed as art objects. The exhibition depicts an astounding array of imagination and creativity of hairstyles from more than 100 people in 25 mostly sub-Saharan countries, including Southern Africa, West Africa, and East Africa (pg. 182). In Sieber and Herreman's catalog, the masks of the Mende and Sowei women of Liberia and Sierra Leone provides an in-depth treatment of the relations between sociality and symbolism while preserving the inherent mystery of Sande society ritual; the gallery also includes an impressive mask with corkscrew braids from Cross River, Nigeria. Through the exhibition, Herreman suggests that the photos and figures reveal that the African sculptor represents hairstyles conceptually rather than mimetically. Hair is also is an expression of the life cycle, which correlates to the hairstyles of youth, as well as to spiritual beliefs and stages of life. In these galleries and photos, the relations between hairstyles and culture are made explicit and the effects of acculturation and change are considered (Sieber and Herreman 2000). The final gallery presented a section of marvelous painting advertising signs from a Ghanaian barbershop. This particular section of the exhibition was virtually the only painting in the show, in contrast to the masks, sculptures, and photographs elsewhere (Sieber and Herreman 2000). The painting suggests a radical disjuncture between older and more modern forms of representation in contemporary Africa. Overall, the exhibition presented a portrayal of Black hair throughout Africa and within African diaspora communities beyond the continent.

By tradition, Black hair has been perceived in a number

of contradictory ways. The outlook of Black hair began in the continent of Africa. During historic times in Africa, hairstyles represented a person's ascribed status. According to some sources, "Hair is the complexity of the social code and it functions as a key ethnic signifier because compared with bodily shape or facial features, it can be changed more easily by cultural practices.... Caught on the cusp between self and society, nature and culture, the malleability of hair makes it a sensitive area of expression" (Mercer, 1994). To others, hair is classified as an indication of racial differences and as a sign of group identity or else of self-identification, political ideology, and social status (Sieber and Herreman 2000). Furthermore, hair is possibly second only to skin color as socially-based on group affiliation; but unlike skin, hair readily adapts itself to human innovation in a host of significant appearances (Sieber and Herreman 2000). In Africa, hairstyles were used to represent a person's marital status, age, religion, ethnic identity, wealth, and rank within the community. For instance, royalty often wore elaborate hairstyles to represent their stature. Hair was also an emblem of fertility. If a person's hair was thick, long, and neat, this signified that they were able to bear healthy children. If someone was in mourning, they would pay minimal attention to their hair (Matshego, 2020).

Due to hair being a part of one's body, ancient communities also believed that hair helped with divine communication. With this belief, hair styling was entrusted to close relatives. It was thought that if a strand of hair fell into the hands of an enemy, harm could come to the hair's owner (Matshego, 2020).

ID 123777904 © Artur Balytskyi | Dreamstime.com

Those who specialized in hair care were highly respected within their communities. Girls were instructed in braiding hair and if they mastered the braiding techniques, then they were encouraged to become hair stylists. Likewise, if their hair was not groomed or otherwise neglected, women were considered to have no morals or class. Along with hair, head wraps/scarves are also significant in Africa. They were traditionally worn by older, usually married women. Head wraps/scarves were a common feature in ceremonies such as weddings and funerals, and they were often worn either for religious and cultural reasons, as fashion statements, or later, even as a symbol of freedom (Fihlani 2016).

When the transatlantic slave trade first emerged, enslaved Africans' heads were shaved before they were sent off to the Caribbean, Latin America, or North America. Although it was said that this shaving was for sanitary reasons, it actually was the first tactic to strip away slaves from their African identity and to lower their status (Ballinger 2007). In addition, slave masters and mistresses often told slave children that their hair texture was "ugly," encouraging them to hate it. A scientist from the 1850s, Peter A. Browne, even claimed that Black and white men must be from two differing species because white men have hair while Black men have wool and not hair on their heads (Ballinger 2007).

Once enslaved, hair also became the matter of labor and was forced to reflect that. For instance, field slaves often hid their hair by wearing wraps, while house slaves had to wear wigs in order to look "decent" rather than offending their masters with the appearance of their natural hair (Thompson 2008; Thomas 2009). Therefore, house slaves were often given time for grooming and slave women were encouraged to iron their hair straight so that it looked more similar to their white counterparts' (Byrd and Tharps 2001). Field slaves, though, were given little or no time to work on their hair. They were often forced to wear their hair wrapped in a scarf hiding the "offensive wool" from whites around them, and jealous mistresses would force enslaved Black women to keep their hair unkempt, humiliating them through by ensuring disease, baldness, or hair breakage (Byrd and Tharps 2001). After a while, slave masters began viewing each other's slaves and judging the master by the condition of all his slaves. As this became common practice, however, the judges didn't evaluate

UNRAVELING THE STORY OF BLACK/AFRICAN HAIR

just the house slaves who were required to look as white in appearance; field slaves were often critiqued as well. As a result, many masters began to allow all their slaves Sundays off for personal usage and proper grooming (Byrd & Tharps 2001). So, on Sundays, women would gather and braid everyone's hair. Furthermore, Sundays would be the day that everyone would "let their hair out" without wearing head wraps. After everyone's hair was styled, the women would attend church and everyone would view each other's hair. All the women's hair would be braided in intricate patterns and designs which would last for the rest of the week, by having their hair hidden under a scarf to keep it nice.

From a certain perspective, then, the hair care rituals that began in Africa are still preserved in the African diaspora (Byrd & Tharps 2001). From one vantage point, though, the head-wrap was also an object of oppression. The Tignon Law enacted by Governor Don Estevan Miro of New Orleans in 1786 reflects this (Everett, 1966 pg. 34). This law prohibited free women of color from displaying too much attention to their attire, so Black women developed the Tignon (Tiyon) as a type of head covering. The Tignon was a large piece of cloth or fabric that is wrapped or tied around the head, to form a kind of turban that resembles a West African Gele. At the time, wearing one was a visible sign of belonging to the slave class, whether the women were actually enslaved or not. On the other hand, the women who were affected by this law did in fact use it to their advantage by using elaborate fabrics and jewels to cover their heads, which allowed them to maintain their standards of fashion and beauty (Brown & Knapp 2005-2006). The Tignon also exhibited their connections to their ancestral homeland Africa. Thus, from another perspective, head wraps also became a vehicle of empowerment and a memento of freedom.

Eventually, as white masters began to force themselves on Black women slaves, multi-racial children grew into women whose hair was considered "good" as it was straighter, softer, and looser in nature and appearance then their Black mothers'. In addition to the appearance of "good" hair, having lighter skin became another pressure on Black and multiracial women to look as white as possible in appearance. However, even those with "good hair" were penalized if it still was not "good" enough. One common story recounts how "Even though some slaves had lighter complexions as many whites, the rule of thumb was that if the hair showed just a little bit of kinkiness, a person would be unable to pass as white. Fundamentally, the hair acted as the true test of Blackness, which is why some male slaves chose to shave their heads to try to get rid of the genetic evidence of their African ancestry, when attempting to escape to freedom" (Byrd and Tharps 2001: 18). Moreover, female slaves started changing their hair from its natural state in an act of self-hatred.

In the 1900s after the emancipation of slavery in the United States, products and tools for kinky hair started to rise in the market. One of the first straightening tools invented was the hot comb, an invention developed by a Frenchman named Marcel Grateau in 1872. It was a way for women with coarse curly hair to achieve a fine straight look. The hot comb hair style had its basis in tools and styles habitually modeled by historical Egyptian women (Byrd and Tharps 2001).

The Significance of Black/African Hair

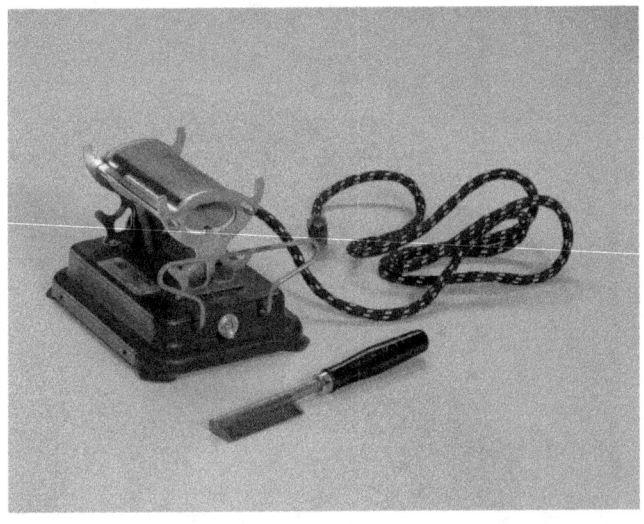

Collection of the Smithsonian National Museum of African American History and Culture, Gift of Linda Crichlow White in honor of her aunt, Edna Stevens McIntyre. CC0

However, it was chemist and entrepreneur Annie Malone who first tested this tool more widely, and her protégé and former employee, Madam CJ Walker, later widened the teeth.

UNRAVELING THE STORY OF BLACK/AFRICAN HAIR

Photograph by: Addison N. Scurlock
Subject of: Madam C.J. Walker
2013.153.8
Photograph of Madam C.J. Walker
ca. 1912
silver and photographic gelatin on photographic paper
H x W: 5 15/16 x 3 15/16 in. (15.1 x 10 cm)
Repro. Credit Line : Collection of the Smithsonian National Museum of African American History and Culture, Gift of A'Lelia Bundles / Madam Walker Family Archives
SI Usage Statement : Not determined

(Chamberlain 2012).

The hot comb quickly became a very controversial invention because many debated whether it was more beneficial or harmful to the Black community. Several African Americans believed that the hot comb would be destructive to the African American community because it made them submissive to the

The Significance of Black/African Hair

'white ideal image' of beauty and marginalized Black/African culture. Others believed that efforts like hair straightening would boost their social and economic status. This dilemma continued throughout the 20th century and even the 21st.

Today, hot combs are still used by many Black beauticians and families as an alternative to chemical hair straightening. Many Black women of other races also still utilize hot combs because this form of straightening is temporary and less damaging to the hair if done correctly.

Another post-slavery invention, following the hot comb, was the creation of hair products for Black women. The woman behind widening the hot comb was the Black self-made millionaire Sarah Breedlove, also known as Madam CJ Walker. After the death of her first husband followed by the stress of her hardships, her hair began to fall out. Like any other individuals who suffer from hair loss, she tried many products that claimed to help her hair growth, but there was no progress. However, when she started using African American businesswoman Annie Turbo Malone's "The Great Wonderful Hair Grower," she began to see results. She also joined

Malone's team of Black women sales agents (Michals 2015). Along with Malone's hair products aiding to her hair growth, Walker started to experiment with her own products that had similar outcomes. During this point Walker had a vision in which she describes, "a big Black man appeared to me and told me what to mix up for my hair. Some of the remedy was grown in Africa, but I sent for it, put it on my scalp, and in a few weeks my hair was coming in faster than it had ever fallen out" (Chamberlain 2012). After the success in treating her hair loss, Walker shared her formula with some friends and found that it was effective for them as well. Walker then decided to go into business, selling hair products to Black

Collection of the Smithsonian National Museum of African American History and Culture, Gift of Linda Crichlow White in honor of her aunt, Edna Stevens McIntyre. CC0

Women, and in doing so, she realized that there were few products available for Black consumers. When Walker married Charles Joseph Walker, the couple was able to set up the Madam CJ Walker Manufacturing Company. Due to Walker's husband's writing skills and his innate talent for marketing, they started issuing advertisements in Black newspapers throughout the United States. Although the Walkers proved to be a successful team, they disagreed as to how much the company should grow. After years of struggling and suffering, Walker wanted her company to grow immensely and divorced her former husband in order to devote herself to the business; however, Charles stayed on as a sales agent for the company (Chamberlain 2012). She continued on with many of the ideas he had passed on to her, including going door-to-door to sell the products. Her hard work paid off and in 1906 she brought her daughter Lelia, a recent college graduate, in to manage the company. While her daughter managed much of the company, Walker traveled across the country and throughout Latin America and the Caribbean marketing existing products and developing new ones. She also wanted to bring more women into the company, desiring to empower them and give them a way of rising above the restraints set by a male-dominated society.

In 1908, Walker started Lelia College in Pittsburgh, Pennsylvania, which taught women how to sell her products door-to-door and by 1910 had more than a thousand sales agents. That same year, Walker moved the company's headquarters to Indianapolis, Indiana and soon the company grew beyond anyone's expectations (Chamberlain 2012). By 1914, Madame CJ Walker became the women now worth more than $1 million, despite the fact she had only had 2 dollars to her name just nine years earlier. Her products ranged from hair conditioners to facial creams, and hot combs made especially for the hair of Black consumers. Soon after she became a millionaire, Walker was able to purchase a 34-room mansion built off of the Hudson River in New York. When she died on May 25, 1919, she was mourned throughout the Black community as a pioneer and a Black industrialist (Chamberlain 2012). For many women of all races, she had served as an inspiration and a role model. Today, her hair products can be purchased at www.mcjwbeautyculture.com and are sold exclusively at Sephora.

Another pioneer in the Black beauty and cosmetic business is Annie Turnbo Malone. Malone was a businesswoman, inventor, and philanthropist, as well as one of the first self-made African American millionaires. Her legacy has been overshadowed by the success of her former employee, Madam C. J. Walker; however, Malone is now beginning to be more widely recognized and given her due justice.

Malone took an interest in hair care at a young age, when she often styled her sisters' and friends' tresses. However, even they warned her not take her dream of starting her own hair care company seriously (Schleier 2018). Annie attended high school in Peoria, Illinois, but she was often sick and missed class. Though she did not graduate, she did discover she was good at chemistry (Engel). Outside of school, Turnbo continued to read about the latest advances in chemistry. While reading an article about an ointment that dairy farmers used to treat the skin of cows' udders, she had an epiphany. Malone purchased some of the ointment from a local drugstore, mixed

UNRAVELING THE STORY OF BLACK/AFRICAN HAIR

Created by: Poro College
Subject of: Annie Malone
Owned by: Lucille Brown
2011.170.18
Souvenir booklet about Poro College Company
1920-1927
ink on paper with cardboard and cord
6 1/4 x 9 7/16 x 1/4 in. (15.9 x 24 x 0.6 cm)
Repro. Credit Line: Collection of the Smithsonian National Museum of African American History and Culture
SI Usage Statement: CC0

in natural ingredients from her herbalist aunt to add a fresh, attractive aroma, and so created a formula that regrew hair in bald patches left by the snake oil concoctions that Black women had used in the past. Unlike these competitors, though, Malone's product could help regrow or straighten Black women's hair without damaging it like the other products then available (Schleier 2018). This new product became known as "The Great Wonderful Hair Grower."

The Significance of Black/African Hair

Created by: Poro College
Subject of: Annie Malone
Owned by: Lucille Brown
2011.170.18
Souvenir booklet about Poro College Company
1920-1927
ink on paper with cardboard and cord
6 1/4 x 9 7/16 x 1/4 in. (15.9 x 24 x 0.6 cm)
Repro. Credit Line: Collection of the Smithsonian National Museum of African American History and Culture
SI Usage Statement: CC0

Malone also expanded her line of hair care and beauty products for Black women to include face powders, cleansing cream, and shampoos. Her haircare and cosmetic line came to be known as Poro (Schleier 2018). After realizing that she needed a larger market in which to sell her products, Malone moved her business to St. Louis in 1902, taking advantage of the way the city's economy was booming in preparation for the 1904 World Fair.

    Due to Malone being a Black woman, she was denied

access to regular distribution channels. As a result, she and her selling agents went door-to-door, giving demonstrations about Poro products (Engel). As a result, business grew steadily. After a positive response at the World Fair, Malone's company Poro went national, attracting Black women from around the US as well as customers from Latin America and the Caribbean (Engel). In 1914, Malone married Aaron E. Malone, a St. Louis school principal who helped her extend the brand by franchising beauty salons around the country. Malone also assured a continued supply of qualified beauticians and salespeople by starting Poro College in 1918. Poro College offered Black women a place to advance themselves, which included courses on etiquette: how to walk, talk, and dress — all to prepare women for the workplace. The facilities also housed Malone's business operations and served as a place for the African American community to gather for various civic functions.

There has been much discussion of how Malone came up with the name Poro. There are theories that she named her company after the West African men's secret society called

The Significance of Black/African Hair

Poro, Purrah, or Purroh in Sierra Leone, Liberia, Guinea, and Cote d'Ivoire. The Poro society is dedicated to discipline and to enhancing the body both physically and spiritually (Little 1948). In another theory, Malone named her college Poro because the name sounded Afrocentric (Schleier 2018). Whatever the actual reason, though, it is evident that by using the name Poro, Mrs. Malone wanted her sales agents and consumers alike to connect with their African ancestry. According to John H. Whitfield, the author of the biography *"A Friend to All Mankind": Mrs. Annie Turnbo Malone and Poro College*, Mrs. Malone's motto was "clean scalps mean clean bodies." In order for a person's hair to thrive, Malone recommended washing it regularly, using a sulfur-based treatment, eating a healthy diet, and practicing scalp massages. Moreover, the Poro system was not based on hair styling so much as it was on scalp hygiene (Nittle 2019). This recommendation continues to be used today as a means of promoting length retention, scalp health, and hair health among Black/African people.

By the end of World War I, Malone was a millionaire

and one of the most successful Black women of her time. She was also extremely generous with her money and helped a variety of African American organizations and charities (Engel). Unfortunately, in 1927, Malone's multi-million dollar was at risk because when her husband filed for divorce he wanted half of her business. The dispute resulted in a settlement of $200,000. After the divorce, Malone moved her business headquarters to Chicago in 1930, but financial troubles continued to follow her. The aftermath of the 1929 stock market crash hit the company hard, as did a series of lawsuits. Despite these financial setbacks, though, Malone remained in business and by the mid-50s had 32 branches of the Poro School throughout the country (Engel). She also continued to support charities in St. Louis and across the nation throughout her lifetime. She died in Chicago on May 10, 1957. Malone is also remembered as a strong believer of giving back. She donated substantial sums to Howard University School of Medicine and the St. Louis Colored Orphans Home (now the Annie Malone Children and Family Service Center), among other charities (Engel).

The Significance of Black/African Hair

In 1920, another type of hair product, the "conk," was created. The name conk is derived from Congolene, which is a hair straightener gel made from lye as well as a popular hairstyle among African American men from the 1920s through the 1960s. This hairstyle was specialized for a man with naturally kinky hair to have it chemically straightened using a relaxer or sometimes the pure corrosive chemical lye; this enabled the newly straightened hair to be styled in exclusive ways. Frequently, the relaxer was prepared at home by mixing lye, eggs, and potatoes (Adams 2005, p. 85). The applier would have to wear gloves and the person to whose hair the mixture was applied also had to have their head fully rinsed after the application, in order to avoid chemical burns. The process of the conk or any hair perms would be painful to the scalp because of the burning sensation from the lye. Conks were often styled as large pompadours, though some men also chose to simply slick their straightened hair back, allowing it to lie flat on their heads. Regardless of the styling, conks required a considerable amount of effort to maintain: a man who had one often had to wear a do-rag of some sort at home, to prevent sweat or other agents from causing his hair to revert to its natural state prematurely. The style also required repeated application of relaxers; as new hair grew in, it also had to be chemically straightened (Conk 2014).

Many of the popular musicians of the early to mid-20th century, including Chuck Berry, Louis Jordan, Little Richard, James Brown, members of The Temptations, and The Miracles, were well known for sporting the conk hairstyle (Adams 2005, p.85). The style fell out of popularity when the Black Power movement of the 1960s took hold and the Afro became a popular symbol of African pride (Adams 2005, p.85). The conk was also a major plot device in Spike Lee's film biography *Malcolm X*, based on Malcolm X's own condemnation of the hairstyle as Black self-degradation in his autobiography because of its implications about the superiority of a more "white" appearance, as well as the pain the process caused and the possibility of receiving severe burns to the scalp (Adams 2005, p. 85). The conk is all but extinct as a hairstyle among African American men today, although more mildly relaxed hairstyles such as the Jheri curl and the S-curl were popular during the 1980s and 1990s. While not involving the use of chemical relaxers, the "wave" style, commonly worn by young African American men and teens in the 2000s, may be considered to be a new version of the conk, in that the wearer's natural hair is waved using pomades and the form of pressing flattened curls into place using a do-rag (Adams, pg.85).

34 years after the conk was invented, an entrepreneur by the name of George E. Johnson Sr. launched his own company, Johnson Products, that focused on the African American male hair care market. The seed money for the company came from a loan of $500 that had been earned as a vacation loan. Within three years, Johnson Products had also found success in the women's hair care market with the development of Ultra Sheen, a revolutionary hair straightener that could easily be used in the home (The History Makers 2003). Over the next few decades, Johnson Products continued to grow, focusing its efforts on not only creating quality products, but also on training cosmetologists on proper usage of these products. In 1964, Johnson also founded Independence Bank, and during the 1960s he became the exclusive sponsor

UNRAVELING THE STORY OF BLACK/AFRICAN HAIR

behind the nationally syndicated dance show Soul Train (The History Makers 2003). In 1971, Johnson Products became the first Black-owned company to be listed on the American Stock Exchange, and that same year, Johnson became the first African American to serve on the board of directors of Commonwealth Edison (The History Makers 2003). In the mid-1980s, more and more competitors began entering the African American hair care industry and the Federal Trade Commission forced Johnson Products to put warning labels on lye-based products—notably, without requiring Revlon to do the same.

Over the course of his career, Johnson received numerous honors. *Ebony* magazine awarded him with its American Black Achievement Award in 1978, and in 1979 he received the public service award of the Harvard Club for the work of the George E. Johnson Foundation and the George E. Johnson Educational Fund. Johnson was active with a number of civic organizations as well, including the Chicago Urban League, the Lyric Opera, Northwestern Memorial Hospital, and Operation PUSH (The History Makers 2003).

Around the same time that Johnson launched his Ultra-

The Significance of Black/African Hair

Sheen product, more Black women and men, especially in the 1960s-70s, began viewing hair as a political statement and a symbol of the Black power movement (Ballinger 2007, p. 65). Hair was used as a resilient strategy against Eurocentric beauty standards (White 2005). Women such as Angela Davis became emblems of power and the struggle to overcome racism and challenge white supremacy. People showed their racial pride by wearing thick tall afros to attempt to alter racist stereotypes that insisted that people with kinky hair are monstrously ugly, undesirable, or even evil (Hooks 1995). Hair became a symbol of power and recognition. However, in the 1990s, afro hairstyles, locs, and braids became a symbol of delinquency for men and once again of lower status for women (Ballinger 2007, p. 65).

Then in the late 1970s-1980s, the rise of the Jheri (Jerry) curl style became a popular hairstyle for Black men and women. The Jheri curl is a hairstyle developed by white chemist and stylist Robert William Redding, who also created hair conditioner and PH-balanced shampoo (Taylor 2013). The Jheri curl was advertised as a low-maintenance wash and wear style, and also as easier to care for than a chemical relaxer. On the flip side, the activator had bad side effects, including the way that the oil would stain clothing, furniture, and anything that it came into contact with. Nevertheless, some of the many celebrities who wore Jheri curls at some point were Michael Jackson, Deion Sanders, Walter Peyton, Eazy E, Samuel L. Jackson, Rick James, Ice Cube, and Eric LaSalle in the film *Coming to America* (Taylor 2013). Along with the Jheri curls, styles such as the flat top, weaves, and the continuing of hair relaxers were very much a part of the 80s.

In the 1980s, too, weaves raised the bar for Black beauty even higher by requiring hair that was not just straight, but also very long (Banks, 2000; Byrd & Tharps, 2001; Tate, 2007). Hair weaving is a process by which synthetic or real human hair is sewn into one's own hair. There are many various ways to wear a weave. A woman may braid her hair and then sew "tracks" (strips of hair) onto the braided hair, or using a bonding method, tracks can be glued to the hair at the root. Furthermore, braid extensions are a similar method in which synthetic hair is braided into a person's own hair, thereby creating an illusion of long hair that can also stay in for a long period of time (Thompson 2008-2009). Straight hair is still the North American norm and is often needed to secure employment for African American women. Some women will go as far as to get micro-braids, which, due to their tiny size, give the appearance of long straight hair.

The reasons why Black women will do this can depend on the generation you ask. According to many scholars, as we have already seen, hair has always been an important factor in defining one's identity (Brownmiller 1984; White 2005; Byrd and Tharps 2001; Patton 2006). For African Americans this is doubly true, as women with straightened hair are still considered the beauty norm in society today. Women of power and upper-class status often wear their hair straightened, and usually not in a natural style, though the length may vary and some even wear braids (Patton 2006). Women who are lower-class more often wear their hair in braids, which is interesting because braids are more expensive than having one's hair chemically straightened and can be more time consuming (Ballinger 2007). Essentially, to African Americans hair defines one's race, one's heritage, and also the self. According to Dione-Rosado (2004), relaxed hair, braids, weaves, and shortly cropped hair are considered more professional in nature, and hence they are more often adopted by middle-class Black women. By contrast, supposed natural hairstyles (i.e., locs and twists) are viewed as more radical hairstyles in the professional world. Therefore, Black hair and hairstyles can be still seen as an indicator of gender, social class, sexual orientation, political views, religion, and even age (Dione-Rosado 2004).

    Researchers Electra Gilchrist and Courtney Thompson discuss how the media permeates society, up to impacting African American women's perceptions of hair. When African American women and girls view hair magazines or commercials that focus on Black hair, they try to emulate the hair styles they see, and the main goal is to achieve what they identify as "good hair" (pg.1). Even though celebrities like T'keyah Crystal Keymáh, Lauryn Hill, Erykah Badu, and India Irie brought about an Afrocentric appeal with their hair and clothes in the 1990s and early 2000s, a lot of Black women still preferred their hair relaxed, in weaves, or using hair-extensions at the time.

Mary's Hair Story

My name is Mary and I am from a rural town in North Carolina. I am a twenty-four-year old Black woman and most recently an elementary school teacher in my hometown. I enjoy traveling, attending fan conventions, and working in the community by educating and volunteering.

Until recently, my hair has always been bothersome. I never knew what to do with it. I was permed pretty early on, and I would either just wear it down or get braids. Once I started college, though, I went natural, so I haven't had a perm in about seven years now. I wore braids consistently, with an occasional "fro" style, for about six-and-a-half of those years. Not only was it tiring to do my hair like this, but also it was expensive and after a while I got tired of these styles too.

When I was younger, I was always interested in locs. I wanted to get them but I didn't really know how and my parents didn't want me to have them. In December 2019, I finally took the leap and got them installed. I am approaching six months with locs now and it has been the best decision! I have loved them from the install and could see myself with them for years to come.

I was relaxed for about a decade. I returned natural on November 1, 2013. Now I love my hair! It's so me. Not much to maintain and a symbol of my pride. It is a part of who I am: non-conforming, bold, and constantly evolving. I think natural hair has become much more popular within the last decade, especially in the professional world. Recent laws have made discrimination by hair illegal; however, it's still very controversial to wear certain styles in particular places. I view natural hair as a wonderful thing, but I do not think any less of permed Black women. It is a choice and shouldn't be seen as a weakness.

LaTonya's Hair Story

Hello, I am LaTonya Renee and I am African American. I was born and raised in Winston-Salem, NC. I never really lived away from the city until I was over forty and then I moved 2 hours away to Raleigh, NC. To be honest, family is my biggest hobby; we get together to cook and play bingo and cards. I also love watching my grandson play football. I enjoy going to empowerment events for women and listening to motivational speakers, and I also love affirmations, plus sharing them and positivity with others. I have a few things that I have always wanted to do that I plan on doing when I just simply schedule the time to do it. I would love to learn to dance (African, modern, tap, and line dance). After COVID-19, my new hobby will be traveling to other countries.

I am a Gen-Xer. Being a part of Generation X always made me feel my hair could NEVER be out of place. During this era, your hair was a huge part of who you were and who you hung out with or not! There were so many hairstyle fads and I was always trying to keep up with all of them. It was taboo not to. Perms and wearing your own hair was the norm at the time, and it wasn't about wearing weaves. I was so good at doing my own hair and making it look like I had been to the salon. In my early 20s I went to school to become a hairstylist. I went to school part-time but never completed the hours to graduate; however, this never stopped me from doing hair for others. I did hair for years in my home (my way of earning part-time income). At one point I was earning more money at home doing hair than I was by going to work at a full-time job.

During my youth, my aunts would always press my hair; once I got to high school, though, I started wearing perms, and I have never turned back since. I have thought about going natural; however, I am too tender headed. I can barely stand for my hair to be braided, and I can't work with heavy-handed beauticians. I've been blessed to have a good grade of thick, healthy hair throughout my life. Until I was 28 years old I had shoulder-length hair, and then one day I decided to change and cut it all off. I have never looked back from that either! The short styles that I wear have really become a signature look for me. I love my hair. I normally wear short hairstyles and, before COVID, would maintain it every other week. Prior to moving to Raleigh, I kept the same hairdresser for approximately 20 years. I take pride in my hair and I am known for wearing short, sassy, classy hairstyles. Since COVID, it has been difficult to maintain the short look, since my hair has grown

UNRAVELING THE STORY OF BLACK/AFRICAN HAIR

out; so I have had my share of braids, crochets, and all the other trendy protective styles. I've only continued to wear these styles because I'm so skeptical of finding a new hairstylist who can do my hair exactly like I am accustomed to wearing it. I am truly ready to get back to the old me with a short, Black, classy conservative look.

Chapter 2

The Commodification of Black Hair

As we continue to explore Black hair, the Black hair care industry also merits recognition and some exploration of its own. As Black consumers continue to embrace their natural hair, the impact of this movement is greatly shaping the Black haircare market, in the US particularly. New research from Mintel reveals that, since 2016, Black consumers has been spending an estimated $2.56 billion on hair care products. As we have already seen, hair is an important aspect of Black culture, so it is not a surprise that the Black hair care industry is worth so much. *Good Hair*, the 2009 documentary by comedian Chris Rock, shone a spotlight on the business of Black hair, particularly the use of relaxers and weaves and the sources of the extensions so many women sew into their hair. Since Rock's revelations about the industry, much has changed in the world of Black hair—but only to an extent. Mintel argues that, with natural hair becoming the new norm, relaxer sales continue to fall. In fact, sales of relaxers in the Black haircare market have plunged 36.6% between 2012-2017 to reach $525 million (Mintel, 2017).

Around 2015-2017, Black consumers' purchase of shampoo increased by 13%, which is the most growth seen among all haircare segments during that time period and accounts for an estimated 19 % of the market. In addition, conditioner sales hold an estimated 19 % of the market as well. On the other hand, styling product sales (30 % market share) remain stagnant with 0.4 % growth in 2017. Styling products have a 30% share in the Black hair care market (Mintel, 2017). According to Mintel reports, 52% of Black consumers use 3-4 haircare products and approximately 50% of Black consumers wash their hair once a week or a few times a month. Within the natural hair community, people often have a day called "wash day," in which time is set aside to complete basic hair maintenance. In fact, Black consumers spend an average of 63.1 minutes on basic hair maintenance on "wash day," compared to just 21.2 minutes if and when they style their hair on an average day (Mintel, 2017).

It is also important to look into the type of hair maintenance that is being done on wash days, because the specifics can vary greatly. For instance, a person may just shampoo and condition their hair, or they may do a shampoo and conditioner, plus a deep conditioner or a protein treatment. Depending on the type of maintenance needed on a wash day, the length of time needed varies. Overall, 49% of Black consumers are more likely to use just 1-2 products when washing and styling their hair, while Black women, regardless of hairstyle, seem to have a product-focused regimen as more than half (52 %) say they use 3-4 haircare products.

"Going natural" is also becoming the norm for many Black consumers, especially among young consumers who are adopting a variation of styles specifically for work and play. Having an interest in chemical-free hair has been focused on achieving healthy hair and having different alternatives for straight hairstyles, instead of using chemical straighteners that alter one's natural hair. The use of heating tools such as a blow dryer or flat iron to achieve straight styles also required the use of heat-protectant products and minimized heat usage, in order to prevent hair from receiving heat damage. As the use of relaxers declines, Black consumers are also becoming more interested in products that help them achieve the desired look without the same old time commitments or skills. Mintel reports that 41% of consumers prefer to use Black hair care brands. In addition, maintaining healthy hair is a priority: two in five (40%) Black consumers say they avoid unhealthy haircare products and three in 10 (29%) avoid unhealthy hair styling techniques (Mintel, 2017). Haircare product performance is vital for Black consumers, as 43% agree that they prefer to use products that will perform as expected. Many also choose to use brands that are created for their specific styling needs, while 41% prefer to use brands for Black hair.

This is especially among those who wear their hair natural, both with heat (54%) and without (51%) (Mintel, 2017). Due to Black consumers abandoning products that contain certain chemicals, many are gravitating toward haircare products and brands that are natural or formulated specifically for Black/African textured hair. These brands address consumers' maintenance according to different hair textures and styling choices. As consumers transition from using relaxers to going chemical-free and wearing natural hair, more companies should take the time to understand consumer's hair textures, challenges and goals, as well as offer solutions that help keep hair healthy and styled as desired. There should also be more extensive education on what ingredients are and how they affect hair. This could be of great value to consumers while searching for products. Currently, regimen-focused product lines and styling products are enjoying the spotlight, while sales on relaxers are declining. Since 2017, Mintel estimated that consumer expenditure on Black haircare totaled $2.54 billion, falling just 0.4 % from the year prior (Mintel, 2017).

Moreover, sales of weaves and wigs also experienced growth because these enable consumers to switch up their looks while also protecting their real hair beneath these hairstyles (Opiah 2014). Mintel reports that nearly six out of 10 Black consumers either wear a wig, weave, or extensions.

A complicating factor here, though, is the increased competition in the Black hair care market, plus the demographics of who owns the supply stores that form such an important part of the Black hair care market (Opiah 2014). Most of these beauty supply stores are owned by non-Black immigrants, many of them Korean. In *Ebony*, Adrienne P. Samuels writes that many Koreans immigrants started their businesses in the Black community in the 1970s and '80s by selling wigs, then weaves and extensions and now everything from perms to clippers. Their businesses were often handed down from father to son or from mother to daughter: children and grandchildren who are second- and third-generation Americans. The flip side is that not too many Black business owners actually own the stores where Black consumers shop; I can attest to Samuels' research personally because while living in Charlotte as a little girl in the late 1990s, the only few Black employers I saw who owned beauty supply stores were Ethiopians, and the rest were Asian. Even fewer Black people manufacture or distribute the goods for beauty products. It's an odd world that has seemingly made everyone but a handful of Black people rich.

One common assumption is that some people think that Black consumers are lazy and they don't want to own their own business (Samuels 2008). Another view is that the US government favors non-Black immigrants with loans and special business favors: the Chris Rock documentary *Good Hair* depicts the situation as a deliberate Asiatic takeover that is being fought at every turn by Black entrepreneurs trying to get a solid piece of the pie (Samuels 2008). Although these companies stand to increase competition within the industry, particularly within the rapidly-growing natural hair category, they're also faced with the fact that Black consumers are more likely to buy products from Black-owned brands. Big business lacks the credibility of smaller brands that are often users of their own products and have built strong relationships with their consumers by sharing their own hair stories (Opiah 2014).

Ten years after the release of Rock's documentary *Good Hair*, numerous African Americans are taking back ownership of the Black-focused beauty supply business. Beauty supply stores have been a part of a multi-billion-dollar industry that has historically locked out African Americans completely, often for long periods of time. According to the Nielson report in 2018, African American women spent more than $54 million in hair care and beauty products in 2017 alone. Since African Americans are the top consumers of the beauty supply business, it is only right that they should have a piece of this ever-growing industry and its benefits as well. As things begin to change, more Black entrepreneurs in the United States and abroad are getting into the haircare and beauty supply store industry, while also making sure to collaborate with other Black peers in the process.

Sam Ennon, president and CEO of The Black Owned Beauty Supply Association reports that "Koreans used to control the market, now they are selling the stores back to us because their kids do not want to take on the store." For the past 15 years, the Black Owned Beauty Supply Association has helped open 450 Black-owned beauty supply stores across the country. Ennon also shared that, "the second and third generation (of Korean Americans) went to college and go into other professions. Moreover, we're very pleased with the future of the Black haircare industry where it's going because more entrepreneurs, more young people are getting into the business." After watching a Korean American owner disrespect an elderly woman and her granddaughter in his store, Chicago native and serial entrepreneur Princess Dempsey didn't hesitate to take immediate steps to assume ownership of the store. In July 2018 Dempsey bought this store and hair inventory, putting the previous owner out of business on the spot. Six months later, after careful planning, she opened Princess Delights Beauty Supply in the Chicago suburb of Westchester, IL (Houseworth-Weston 2018). This interesting yet profitable trend opens doors for the Black community and tackles the continuous racial profiling that many of us have experienced or witnessed while shopping in Asian-owned stores.

    Another significant piece of the Black hair care history

are natural hair entrepreneurs, who are beginning to influence more and more of this billion-dollar industry. Many natural hair entrepreneurs started off on YouTube, at home, in hair salons, or at natural hair meet-up groups before becoming a big business. Miko and the late Titi Branch owners of Miss Jessie's are just a few examples among many. Titi spent months of experimentation in the kitchen of their Brooklyn brownstone until she finally perfected the blend that would come to be known as Curly Pudding. Curly Pudding was a great discovery at the time because in 2003 there were very few hair products for Black women with kinky, curly, or wavy hair. Ms. Miko Branch states that "There was nothing like [Curly Pudding] in the early 2000s. It was really transformative." The product line Miss Jessie's was one of the pioneering brands in the natural hair industry, a once-grassroots segment of the beauty world that's now a multi-million-dollar product line sold in retailers across the country.

Another natural hair entrepreneur is the founder of Alikay Naturals, Rochelle Graham-Campbell. About ten years ago, Graham-Campbell started off as a YouTube beauty vlogger, along with many other titles. She posted several vlogs per week, which she has described as: "I did not have a lot of time, but I made the time by sacrificing other things in my life." Following a $100 investment, she purchased the materials and ingredients needed to make her very first natural hair product, an Essential 17 hair growth oil. Currently, Graham-Campbell and her husband Desmond are operating Alikay Naturals, a beauty and lifestyle natural hair brand now available at many retail stores nationwide. She also has her own manufacturing facility, and Alikay Naturals is currently sold in 150 independent retail locations worldwide, including in France, Netherlands, the United Kingdom, Jamaica, and Bermuda as well as the US.

Another natural hair entrepreneur who deserves time in the spotlight is Julian R. Addo. Addo has over 25 years' experience as a professional hair stylist. While attending a natural hair event in 2012 in NYC, Addo became inspired and launched Bella Kinks. Within the natural hair care world, Addo was concerned with the unrealistic representation of natural beauty in the media, particularly for multicultural men and women. She felt that there wasn't any top-shelf, aesthetically pleasing products by Black people for Black people, and in October 2017 she started her Adwoa Beauty natural haircare line to address this lack. In the Akan ethnic group of Ghana and Côte d'Ivoire, Adwoa is a name given to girls born on a Monday. The name means "one who is philosophical, determined, and filled with intense desire to endure," which reflects Addo's approach to hair care too. Adwoa Beauty displays the merging of care for African hair and African beauty with design, marketing, arts, and transparency. In addition, the company represents Addo's own Liberian and Ghanaian heritage. There is an Adwoa Beauty show room based in Dallas, Texas, which gives people the opportunity to view the products as well as a meeting with a specialized team member who will guide them through the process of achieving their own hair routines at home. The show room also offers fun events and natural hair gatherings.

Addo has created top events, expos, and digital media services with some of the biggest brands in the industry. She has also landed Sally Beauty as a client in 2015, leading to the launch of bella kinks media llc, where Addo continues to consult with brands to provide digital strategy and market insight to improve business. To add on the success of Adwoa Beauty, Addo selected Sephora as her company's retail partner. Addo felt that Sephora's superior leadership and dominance in the prestige beauty market complemented the reasons she had created her own brand. Addo states, "Because [when] I was shopping for skincare and makeup at Sephora, I always imagined Adwoa Beauty sitting on the shelves there. I didn't see it anywhere else but Sephora" (reported by Brown, 2020). Another reason why Addo selected Sephora as a business partner is because there aren't many Black/African or multi-ethnic hair care brands in the prestige beauty sphere. What brands forget to realize is that "there are consumers [who] enjoy modern packaging and branding, great customer service, and are willing to pay a little bit more for products that give you the best results" (reported by Brown, 2020). Addo could provide this through the partnership between Adwoa Beauty and Sephora.

UNRAVELING THE STORY OF BLACK/AFRICAN HAIR

Another naturalista entrepreneur who should be mentioned is Carolina Contreras, a.k.a. Miss Rizos. Contreras plays a conspicuous role with regards to the Afro-Latinx (Latinx) community as they embrace their natural hair. Like many Black peers, Contreras's hair was relaxed as a child, when the idea was to obtain "manageability" or "to be more presentable in society." That changed when she moved back to her native country, the Dominican Republic. Contreras decided to do the big chop (BC), which means cutting of all of the relaxed ends from hair (Another way to return natural is transitioning, where you let your hair grow out and gradually cut off the relaxed hair. In order to work with the two different textures, you can do twists outs, braid outs, roller sets, double strand twists, or braids, then roll your ends with curling rods). Contreras has described returning natural as a process, stating that "I had maybe an inch of curls on my head and it was obviously a very dramatic and drastic change to go from very, very long hair to having it all gone and then a completely different texture that I didn't even recall having before. It was a beautiful process of learning how to love and care for my hair, and in essence learning how to love and care for myself" (reported by Shatzman, 2018).

In 2011, Contreras created her blog Miss Rizos, where she shared information and resources in Spanish about caring for afro-curly hair. There is also a history within the Latinx community where hair that is kinky, curly, afro-like, or coarse is "Pelo Malo" (Bad hair). On the other hand, hair that is straight, or with a looser curl or wave pattern, is "Pelo Bueno" (Good hair). Miss Rizzos has refuted this argument by coining the phrase "Yo Amo Mí Pajón," which means "I love my big afro/curly hair." Pajón is a voluminous plant, but in the Dominican Republic, the word is also used as slang to refer to big hair (Contreras 2017). Contreras used this slogan to promote self-love and beauty within the Afro-Latinx natural hair community.

Adding on to her Miss Rizzos platform, in 2014 Contreras opened up her first salon, also called Miss Rizzos, in the Dominican Republic. The idea evolved from the need to have a space dedicated specifically to curly hair care without the application of chemicals or heat. Miss Rizzos became the first all-curly hair salon in a country that still holds the belief that straight hair is beautiful and natural curls are Pelo Malo (Bad hair). Contreras, along with her salon team, allowed for the Miss Rizzos salon "to become a social enterprise with an innovative, diverse and dynamic team who through beauty, education and empowerment hope to continue changing the world one curl at a time" (Contreras 2018). Contreras has since taken another step by opening a second Miss Rizzos salon in New York City. This came about due to women and girls flying to the Dominican Republic just to visit her salon, Contreras states. She reports that "No one is giving the curly service and experience the way that we do. I almost feel like it's a disservice to not bring it to different places, especially where I have so many supporters" (reported by Diaz 2019). The second location offers the same experience as her salon in the Dominican Republic. Miss Rizzos chose for her salon to be in the Washington Heights area, also known as the "Little Dominican Republic." Contreras further states that "the mission isn't just to slay your strands, but also to pass along knowledge about styling to each client. Salons pride themselves on the stylists being the experts...For us, we're trying to make you the expert" (reported by Diaz 2019).

Just as in any form of entrepreneurship, entrepreneurs throughout the natural hair care world strive for their company to become a high-profit business: the million-dollar or billion-dollar valuation is a dream for many entrepreneurs. This dream became a reality for the founders of Sundial Brands, Liberian-born Richelieu Dennis and his mother Ms. Mary Dennis. For several years, the major corporation Unilever, an Anglo-Dutch consumer goods company, had tried to get in contact with Dennis for a business proposal but has been unsuccessful. Unilever desperately wanted to buy the New York City-based Sundial, a $240 million maker of shampoos, conditioners, and lotions targeted at African diaspora customers under brands such as SheaMoisture and Nubian Heritage. For 20 years, Mr. Dennis avoided these meetings because he wanted to keep full control of his business. In May 2017, Dennis finally agreed to meet with Unilever executives, following encouragement from his friends. Prior to executing this deal, Dennis had a list of terms he wanted, and he figured that Unilever would not compromise. The main one is that he wanted to keep control of his company with no strings attached. Surprisingly, Unilever said yes to everything. Then, to demonstrate sustainability, the Unilever execs laid out their supply chain in Africa. Unilever offered an estimated $1.6 billion for Sundial—a rich sum, especially given that Dennis and his mother Ms. Mary who had cofounded the company with him in 1991, still owned 51% of the company. From this deal, Dennis and his mother received an estimated $850 million fortune. "It was really one of these magical moments," said Dennis, "That was the moment I knew this was the right thing to do." Seven months after that fateful business dinner, Unilever announced its acquisition of Sundial, making Dennis and his mother two of the wealthiest Black entrepreneurs in the world.

    During the early years of Sundial's being, Dennis didn't take outside money, as he grew from a Harlem street vendor to supplying chains like Target and Whole Foods. He did this by riding the boom in natural beauty products—a segment that barely existed 30 years ago but is now a $14.8 billion global industry—and by learning how to scale. Currently, Dennis is working on expanding Sundial products to Africa, Europe, and South America. He has been traveling to those continents extensively, in order to gain a better understanding of the market and customers' needs there. In addition, the company is expanding manufacturing outside the company's Long Island headquarters into areas including Brazil, Nigeria, and South Africa. The company will continue investing a portion of its sales into communities and efforts to improve the lives of those in its supply chain, including more than 20,000 Ghanaian women.

Dennis personally bought *Essence* magazine from Time Inc. for an unrevealed amount, as a result making the magazine fully Black-owned again. Dennis has mentioned that, "What we're doing with *Essence* is not very different from what we've done with Sundial. And that is to serve Black women deeply, to serve women of color in a way that no one else has thought about. In a way that's authentic to who they are, in a way that's dedicated to them (reported by Berg 2019)."

Another business venture Dennis has undertaken was purchasing Madame CJ Walker's 34-room mansion in Irvington, NY, the famous Villa Lewaro. He plans on turning the legendary beauty pioneer's estate into a center of excellence for Black women in business (Hill 2019). More specifically, Dennis plans to convert the 28,000-square-feet residence into a "learning institute, or think tank, to foster entrepreneurship for present and future generations," particularly geared toward helping women entrepreneurs (Hill, 2019). He also provides funding opportunities for women of color who are entrepreneurs: his New Voices Fund has invested $30 million, out of $100 million raised, in brands like Honey Pot (plant-based feminine hygiene products) and the McBride Sisters Collection (a wine company).

During the 1990s and early 2000s, natural hair companies catered to and were largely run by a small community of Black women embracing their natural hair. According to research firm Mintel, natural hair has now hit the mainstream: 71% of Black adults in the U.S. wore their hair naturally at least once in 2016. Not to mention, Black consumers spent an estimated $2.56 billion on hair care products in 2016. Given this growth and value, it is no surprise that others are willing to get into this market. Investments from beauty industry giants have also helped natural hair products move from specialty stores to the shelves of major retailers such as Target, Wal-Mart, and CVS — making it convenient for Black customers to get their hands on products that were once difficult to locate. On the flip side, though, this is also forcing independent Black-owned companies to compete with corporations that long ignored the natural hair market, resulting in sometimes uncomfortable changes for customers and business owners alike.

UNRAVELING THE STORY OF BLACK/AFRICAN HAIR

Jasmine's Hair Story

My name is Jasmine Devine. I was born and raised in the U.S., but I have a mixed ethnic background. My mom is Irish, Puerto Rican, and Native American, while my dad was African American and Native American.

Growing up, I absolutely hated my hair! Especially during middle school, because at that point my mom was mostly still doing my hair and most of the hairstyles that she knew how to do were seen as childish and definitely not cool. It got to the point where people in school would make fun of my hair and unfortunately it was mostly Black kids. Although I went to a predominantly white school, I lived in a predominantly Black neighborhood, and back then most of the Black girls either went to the salon or had family members who could do really cute styles in their hair. But for the most part, my curly 'fro was seen as undone, unkept, or messy. So, it was either keep it that way or go with the big braids with colorful bows and barrettes that my mom would put in my hair.

I am not ungrateful, though! I appreciate my mother's efforts very much, because she and almost every woman in her family all have very long, naturally straight hair. I, on the other hand, have very thick and curly hair. So, my mom mostly learned how to do my hair through trial and error. All she knew was that she wanted my hair to be healthy and keep its texture. She never gave me a perm or put heat to it, and she only used a few products because she didn't want anything to damage my hair. She would also watch when other women (mostly Black) would do other little girls' hair that was coarser like mine; she'd see what they did and what products they used. Then when she felt like she could do it too, she'd give it a try. When my mom was taking care of my hair, it was thick and reached down to the middle of my back.

Around 10th grade I began to flat iron and straighten my hair. This was mostly because when I was still in middle school, I asked my sister to start doing my hair. She was really good at doing the "cute" hairstyles that I liked so much, but unfortunately the products that she used made my hair break off! In 9th grade, she also ended up bleaching and dying my hair. Needless to say, my hair was never the same again after that. So when 10th grade rolled around, I started doing my own hair. The first thing that I learned how to do was to flat iron it. This seemed like it was pretty easy to do and I wanted my hair to look long again. Unfortunately, at that point I still wasn't really comfortable wearing my natural curly hair and even when I did, I would kill it with gel and/or hairspray.

Now that I'm 30 years old, I've had a long time to learn to love my natural hair texture and I've come to really appreciate it. I haven't dyed my hair or put heat to it in almost 3 years now, and I mostly use organic products to care for it. I actually prefer to have my natural hair out now, unlike when I was younger, and I mainly use 100% organic coconut oil in my hair now because I'm trying to undo all of the damage that was done to it over the years.

When it comes to the natural hair movement, I look at it like any other movement or cause. Basically, I realize that not everyone will support it or be a part of it for the same reasons. I would like to believe that most people have gone natural as an act of self-love, but no matter what their reasons might be, I'm just happy to see people finally embracing their natural hair.

UNRAVELING THE STORY OF BLACK/AFRICAN HAIR

TD's Hair Story

My name is TD and I'm from Eastern NC: the 252, to be exact. I'm from a rural area, and most of my family's roots are here as well. I love to read, cook, and experiment with my natural hair, so those would be my favorite hobbies. To be honest, I never really thought about my hair that much growing up, outside of not liking the dated styles my mom kept giving me. I think this may have a little to do with the area that I was in. Natural hair wasn't a norm where and when I was growing up. I don't even think I heard the term until I went to college. I had my hair relaxed and pressed all the way up until I was in college. I actually started to get upset about getting relaxers when I got to high school because of the damage it did to my scalp via chemical burns. I ended up with traction alopecia, and I didn't even know this condition had a name until I was an adult.

I went natural in 2008. In the beginning this was due to required rules for an organization I was joining, where members couldn't get relaxers. I ended up not getting a relaxer for about six months, then after that decided I wanted to give my natural hair a try. After transitioning for about six more months, I ended up cutting off my remaining relaxed hair and I have been fully natural ever since.

My relationship with my hair is so much better as an adult. I didn't realize until recently that I resented the fact that I was given relaxers and didn't understand the damage it was doing to my hair. Going natural forced me to learn about my hair and truly learn to love it. In the "Big Chop" stage where

UNRAVELING THE STORY OF BLACK/AFRICAN HAIR

I had my TWA (teeny weeny afro), I had to learn to love my face and features because I no longer had my hair to hide them. I've now been natural for about 12 years and I will NEVER go back. I love the versatility of my hair, its uniqueness, and the fact that it is a physical representation of my culture. I love the fact that the natural hair community exists, but I am disheartened at the way it perpetuates texturism and colorism. While I am often complimented on the texture of my hair (loose curls, think 3c/4a curl pattern), I recognize that part of this has to do with the way that certain hair textures (like kinkier 4c) are stigmatized.

  I also think that natural hair can never be a trend, since it is a physical embodiment of our Black culture. In a way I guess it is an act of self-love, especially here in the US where the Eurocentric ideal of beauty (long, straight, blonde hair) is the antithesis of Black people's natural hair. Growing up, I didn't see a lot of Black people wearing their natural hair, but it's so common now. That's the part I enjoy the most about the natural hair movement/community: we are normalizing our culture. At the same time, though, we need to make sure that this isn't focused on representing only a specific type of "natural."

UNRAVELING THE STORY OF BLACK/AFRICAN HAIR

Chapter 3

The Natural Hair Movement of the 21st Century

Afro-textured hair is common among certain populations in Africa, the African diaspora, Oceania, and in some parts of South and Southeast Asia. Today, the natural hair movement is focused on encouraging African women and women of African descent to "return natural" and embrace the health and beauty of their hair. Unlike the Black Power movement in the 1960s and 1970s, when returning natural was more of a political statement and revealed a sense of Black/African pride, today's movement is more about self-acceptance, cultural connections, and pride as Black women stop using chemicals and chemical processes to straighten or relax their hair. Key changes in returning or "going" natural include a desire for authenticity, as well as the efficacy and increasing availability of products on the market that specifically cater to natural and/or transitioning hair.

The reason this movement is often called "returning" natural is because Black women are getting back to the hair textures that God blessed us with when we were first born. However, it's also a move that can be fraught with confusion, missteps and sometimes pain, as the 2009 Chris Rock documentary *Good Hair* has attested to. For a start, many women born with Afro-textured hair have not seen their natural texture since childhood. Even some who are acquainted with the texture of their untreated tresses are not comfortable styling their hair in ways that they believe are fashionable and appropriate for them. Figuring out which of the countless hair-care tools and products on the market might work can make the undertaking even more overwhelming.

The Natural Hair Movement of the 21st Century

One of the most intriguing changes in the Black hair market is the notable change that the natural hair movement has had on the Black beauty aesthete. As "naturalistas" overflow social media networks like YouTube, Tumblr, Facebook, and Instagram documenting their natural hair journeys, experimenting with different hairstyles, and scrounging for hair inspiration from natural hair icons and sites dedicated to Black hair; the kinky curly-haired beauty has become a figure other women aspire to be (Opiah 2014).

    Thanks to this growing visibility, more women are buying curls and kinks and weaving them into their own hair. A new extension hair line, The Heat Free Hair Movement, specializes in kinky, curly, and coiled weaves. Their goal is to offer protective hair style options for women both with and without natural hair at the moment (Opiah, 2014). Another popular type of hair style is crochet braids, which have been around since the 1990s. As opposed to the crochet style of the 1990s, though, the textures used today have a more natural appearance, and can include faux locs, twist and braid-outs, flexi-rod sets, or even Senegalese twists (Antonia, 2018). Similar to the hair weaving process, crochet braids involve cornrowing all hair back, but then from there, adding the crochet hair bit-by-bit using a crochet needle (or bobby pin). Next, you slide the needle under the cornrow (latch closed), and finally, open the latch, hook the hair onto the needle, and close the latch. With this style, the crochet looks a lot more like someone's own hair, especially if it is styled like a rod set, twist, or braid outs (Antonia, 2018). In the documentary

The Natural Hair Movement of the 21st Century

Good Hair, Chris Rock created a parody of himself selling afro-textured hair, and it seemed like consumers and sellers preferred straighter or looser weaves. After the documentary's release, many women with relatively tighter curls began purchasing weaves or wigs that complemented their natural hair texture better.

Throughout the natural hair movement of the 21st century, we cannot deny how YouTube has played a pivotal part in encouraging Black women and girls to return natural. In 2009, YouTube was just starting to become the huge social media site that we know today. At the time, though, YouTube was still growing: it expanded ads to seven different formats, signed a partnership with Disney, promoted video launches, and hit more than 1 billion hits per day. It also started to become an explosive beauty tutorial scene, including a market that leaned toward natural Black hair (Meyerson 2019). YouTube natural hair vlogs emerged to provide a counter-narrative on "do it yourself" (D.I.Y) hair care practices, specifically for highly textured hair. More women were also choosing to create their own hair products using all-natural ingredients such as apple cider vinegar for shampoo and then mayo, egg, and honey for deep conditioners. Natural oils like Extra Virgin Olive Oil (EVOO) or Extra Virgin Coconut Oil (EVCO) were also used for the scalp or applied to Shea butter mixes to create homemade moisturizers. Within the natural hair movement those who create their own products are often called "kitchen hair chemists," the new Madam CJ Walkers, or the new Annie Malones.

In general, YouTube and the Internet have played an important role in the growth of the natural hair movement,

allowing more women to gain access to information and inspiration for natural hair care (Opiah 2014). Consequently, more women have begun foregoing hair stylists for their own self-styling and care. Recently the natural hair site Black Girl Long Hair asked their readers: "When it comes to natural hair, are you DIY (do-it-yourself) or do you depend on natural stylists?" In response to this informal survey, 47% said that they'd gone DIY, 23% said they had tried DIY methods but are struggling, 25% reported that they went to a stylist on occasion, and only 5% said they still use stylists regularly.

While Black women vloggers demonstrate product selections while detangling, shampooing, moisturizing, and styling their tightly coiled hair on camera, they are also using their own lived experiences, as both peers and experts to their viewers (Neil and Mbilishaka 2019). Natural hair vloggers also touch on self-love and mental and physical health while maintaining healthy and stylish natural hair. Some prominent natural hair vloggers include Patrice Grell Yursik, who goes by Afrobella and has been called the "godmother of brown beauty," and Tamara Floyd, whose Twitter profile describes her as "O.G. Natural Hair Blogger 2008." Both women were among the first natural hair vloggers and bloggers, and both are still active in the beauty and natural hair communities. In 2011, Afrobella partnered with MAC Cosmetics and released "All Of My Purple Life," a lip gloss she created; Floyd still runs an incredibly thorough natural hair information website called Natural Hair Rules (Meyerson 2019).

Many of these vloggers also fill voids in the information available to those trying to learn about their natural hair. For instance, another natural hair vlogger, Whitney White (Naptural85), was inspired to start vlogging after she realized that her hair texture was different from what she'd expected once she went natural. She has said that "I was expecting my hair to have afro texture, like most of the other vloggers I was following, so when my hair came out and it was in an in-between texture consisting of small, tight coils and kinks, I wasn't sure how to style it. I might as well share what I'm learning since I wasn't seeing the same hair texture as me," (reported by Meyerson 2019). Her first video, entitled "My Natural Hair Journey," took viewers from her early childhood

The Natural Hair Movement of the 21st Century

to the then-present (2009), when she began growing out her natural hair. Content creator Jouelzy, whose hair is 4C, has also observed that she hadn't seen many examples of hair with a texture like hers, and that is why she also started doing natural hair videos: to fill that void. Reviewing wigs was also a big part of Jouelzy's practice as well (Meyerson, 2019.)

Throughout the early years of YouTube natural hair vlogging, vloggers brought awareness to the many textures of Black hair, including explaining what those textures are, plus how to care for and style them. The spectrum of textures ranges from type 1 straight, to 2 wavy, 3 curly, and 4 kinky/coily. These hair classifications came from hair stylist Andre Walker, who was Oprah's hair stylist for 25 years. While this hair chart is now freely available on the internet, it first appeared in Walker's book *Andre Talks Hair!* The Internet has definitely made it easier to find this information, though. Along with using social media as a platform for educating others about natural hair, online spaces can also offer social support for those in the natural hair community. Social support is a communicative process that offers a sense of reassurance and validation (Keating, 2013, as cited in Ellington, 2014). Keating argues that there are subcategories of social support, which include educating others as well as offering advice and empowerment (as cited in Ellington, 2014). African American women have often felt that the social support from naturalistas on social media has influenced their decision-making in regards to returning natural or caring for their tresses (Goswami, Kobler, Leimeister, & Kremar, 2010, as cited in Ellington, 2014).

While there is certainly support online for learning how to care for natural hair, this is also a place to discuss the downsides and setbacks that can come with it. In the *New York Times* article "'Going Natural' Requires Lots of Help," naturalista Maeling Murphy explains that her mother and sisters inspired her to return natural, so she started to transition away from using chemical products (Bey 2011). Unfortunately, four months later she decided to relax her hair again because she just didn't know how to go about her natural hair journey.

For the most part, though, those who were tired of their hair being chemically treated and wanted to return natural could easily start searching YouTube for inspiration, instructions, and other people who have made peace with their kinks and curls. Murphy said that watching videos on YouTube inspired her to pick up the camera herself and create a YouTube channel, Natural Chica. She hoped others would learn from her, saying that "I wanted to contribute to the wealth of information that's out there" (Bey 2011). She's also able to earn some wealth of her own this way: she has a corresponding blog, NaturalChica.com, that she's been able to sell advertising on and make more than a minimum-wage job would bring her (Bey 2011).

Another early natural hair vlogger is Kim Love, who goes by the name Kimmaytube. Love left a six-figure management consulting career to devote herself full-time to making how-to videos on natural hair (she posts a weekly show that includes fashion tips) and selling hair products, tools, and accessories through an online store, LuvNaturals.com. One video, which was about how to make hair conditioner with castor oil and aloe vera juice, got around a million hits. Love adds that, "very few people are talking about the science of our hair and how to handle this fiber that can grow long with the right treatment. People are debating about products, but I'm trying to show the tools and techniques that will work for our hair. Stylists, products, educators; this is a big industry and there's room for everyone. More and more Black women are wearing their hair natural, and hopefully kinky hair will [become] the standard" (Bey 2011).

Even within the natural hair community, though, it can be so easy to get caught up in steps like achieving length that we forget about the ultimate goal, which is healthy hair. Early YouTube influencers like Harmony Knight (ILoveMyFro) not only shared what products they were using for their hair, but also educated viewers on how to maintain and care for their natural hair. Knight returned natural in 2006, after finding that her relaxed hair was being damaged. When she initially did her BC (Big Chop), she didn't intend to go natural: she was only planning for a TWA (Teeny Weeny Afro) and then once her hair grew out, she would relax it again. To her surprise, though, Knight found that "everyone loved her TWA until she reached the awkward stage within her natural hair journey" (Knight

2011). Like many women and girls who return natural, Knight found herself trying to learn her hair's natural texture because it have been relaxed for so many years that she no longer knew what it was. Despite these challenges, though, Knight was determined to care for her natural hair. She has said that "the hurtful comments, stares, and downright hatred for natural hair, made me realize that being my natural self was a problem!" (Knight 2011)! This motivated her to start her YouTube channel and natural haircare line, I Love Fro (https://www.ilovemyfro.com/), in 2008. According to Knight, the purpose of her hair care line is "to help my fellow sisters on their natural hair journey to avoid the pitfalls, gain the confidence and lose the 'good hair' mentality" (Knight 2011).

In a particular video called "Oils are not Moisturizers," Knight discusses a common misconception about hair oils (coconut, olive, grapeseed, avocado, Jamaican black castor, pure shea butter, etc.), which are sealants and not moisturizers. In the video, Knight mentioned that there were viewers who were reaching out to her in regards to combating dry hair, and when she asked them what they were using for styling, they listed only oils but not moisturizers. Following that experience, she made this video, in which she explained that applying oil to a dry hairstyle won't moisturize your hair: it has to be applied to wet hair, and then once the oil is added on the wet hair, it will seal in the moisture. Knight followed up with an easy way to determine whether a styling moisturizer has water as an ingredient. For example, Knight compared her I Love My Fro shea butter whip product to pure shea butter. Her shea butter whip product includes pure shea butter, distilled water, essential oils, and preservatives. Knight applied the shea butter whip to a section of her hair, and she showed how moisturized that section of her hair became because water is the key ingredient of the whip. On the other hand, she took another section of her dry hair and applied pure shea butter to it. While viewing the video, the pure shea butter just sat on top of her hair and didn't moisturize her cuticles. However, when she spritzed water on that section and then applied the pure shea butter atop that, it worked as a sealant to keep the moisture in her hair.

    Adding on to Knight's concept of tackling dry hair

is using either the LOC (Liquid/Leave-in Oil Cream) or the LCO (Liquid/Leave-in Cream Oil) methods. Liquid refers to water, whether from freshly washed hair or from a water-based product like a leave-in conditioner. Once water has been applied, Knight recommends adding of essential oil to your hair, which helps with sealing in the moisture from the water that was added in the first step. Finally, there is the "C" or cream step, where you add a moisturizer like a smoothie or butter. This final step ensures that hydration has been retained in the hair shaft (Moore, 2019). Throughout the natural hair community, some with natural hair prefer the LCO method (Liquid/Leave-in Cream Oil).

Naturalista AseaMae Beauty wrote an article about trying both methods. Her reason for doing the LCO method is that "you don't want to the oil to seal your cuticle prior to adding the moisturizer into the hair. The cream adds moisture to the hair, which penetrates the hair shaft. If the cuticles are sealed, the moisturizer will just sit on top of your hair" (AseaMae, 2019). In addition, when she tested both methods on different sides of her hair, she attested that her hair remained moisturized when using both methods. However, by day three, she observed that the part of her hair with the LOC method was more moisturized as opposed to the side with the LCO. Those with natural hair should test out which method works best for them, and should also be aware of products that might affect the timeframe of this moisturizing. Furthermore, naturals should take note that both methods may result in giving your hair a greasy feel; however, there is always the option to go for a lighter oil. Overall, both methods are good because they increase moisture retention (AseaMae, 2019).

Along with being natural, there are times when Black women might want to wear their hair straight, though without altering their texture. A healthier alternative for stretched hair is African hair threading or hair banding. African threading has been a haircare routine for centuries throughout Sub-Saharan Africa (BB, 2016). The style consists of wrapping sectioned hair in cotton, rubber, silk, or wool threads (Okoroafor, 2017). This technique helps to straighten the hair without using a blow dryer or flat iron. Hair threading also helps with growth because it is a protective style in which the hair is wrapped, which leads to less manipulation of the strands. Banding simply uses hair ties to around each hair section to achieve the banding style, while keeping the ends open ensures curls remain intact at the bottom (Arlexis, 2017). When creating the African threading or banding style, consumers should keep in mind to not do the styles extremely tight because if done so, this can lead to thinning of hair edges. The practice of African threading has been preserved in some African diaspora communities as well. Those who are interested in learning how to do African threading styles should take a look at YouTube natural hair vlogger Nadine's page called Girls Love Your Curls. Nadine gives viewers instructions on how to do African hair threading and discusses the history of it. In addition, she shows how she threads both her own hair and her daughters', demonstrating how to create beautiful African thread hair styles.

    While discussing the natural hair movement, it would be remiss not to discuss the dreadlock and locked (Loc'd) community. Although both "dreads" and "locks" link to the same word, "dread locks," there is a difference between the two terms when they're separate like this. Dreads or dread locks are a hair style that involves sculpting one's hair into ropes (Kira). There are several ways to making this style, which include back combing, rolling, or braiding. On the other hand, locks are created by coiling, braiding, twisting, or palm rolling. The hairstyle is easy to accrue when hair locks naturally (Kira). Dreads and locks both differ in reference to perception and personal experiences (Gabbara, 2016).

    Historically, too, "dread locks" and "locks" can be traced to different civilizations. Chimere Faulk, natural hair stylist and owner of Dr. Locs, reports that "Regardless of race or culture, you will find a connection to having dread locks for spiritual reasons" (reported by Princess Gabbara, 2016). In ancient Egyptian times, pharaohs wore locs: the hairstyle has been found depicted on tomb carvings, drawings, and other artifacts. Some mummified bodies that have been exhumed also still have their locs intact, thousands of years later (Gabbara, 2016). In present times, there are some Horn of Africa ethnic groups, such as the Afar, Asdago, and Dayta, who wear their hair locked (Black Girl Long Hair 2015). Their locks are similar to those of the Egyptian pharaohs, as are their facial features. In addition, the Hamar women wear locks and maintain them using a mixture of butter and red ochre (Black Girl Long Hair 2015). Dating back to 2500 B.C., the Vedas—Hinduism's oldest scriptures—illustrate the Hindu god Shiva wearing locs, or "Jataa" as they are called in Sanskrit (Ashe 2015).

This hairstyle has also been a symbol of power. Samson, a figure from ancient Biblical times, is a recognizable example. An angel appeared to Samson's mother and declared that she would give birth to a son and instructed that she must never cut his hair. The angel also prophesied her son would someday rescue Israel from the Philistines (New Living Translation Judges, 13:5-6). More to the point of this history, though, Samson's locks were said to give him the ability to rip apart the jaws of an attacking lion with his bare hands (New Living Translation, Judges 14:6). He also had the strength needed to snap the ropes tied around his hands when the Philistines attempted to hold him captive, and then used a jaw bone of a dead donkey to kill over a thousand

UNRAVELING THE STORY OF BLACK/AFRICAN HAIR

Philistines (New Living Translation, Judges 15:14-16). When Sampson fell in love with Delilah, the Philistines told her to entice Samson to tell her what made him so strong and how he could be overpowered (New Living Translation, Judges 16:5). Delilah asked Samson three times to reveal to her what made him extremely strong, and he answered in riddles three times, leaving her to try tying him up with seven new bow strings, new ropes, and even weaving his hair into fabric. However, those different acts never weakened him (New Living Translation, Judges 16:6-15). After being nagged by Delilah, Samson finally disclosed his secret: at birth he had been dedicated to God as a Nazarite, and if his head was shaved, he would lose his power (New Living Translation, Judges 16:17). Delilah realized Samson's truth and lulled Samson to sleep with his head in her lap before calling in a man to shave off the seven locks of his hair. Samson's strength left him once his locks were shaved off (New Living Translation, Judges 16:18-20). The Philistines captured him, bound him with bronze chains, and forced to grind grain in prison (Holy Bible, New Living Translation, Judges 16:20-21). But before long his hair began to grow back. The Philistine asked for Samson to amuse them, so he was brought out to the temple, where he placed his hands on the two center pillars that held up the temple and prayed for strength one last time. When God answered his prayer, he pushed and the temple crashed down, killing more people in that one act than he had during his entire lifetime (New Living Translation, Judges 16:30).

Pan-African intellectual Marcus Garvey is often credited with connecting locs to Jamaica. Garvey is best known as the founder of the Rastafari Movement, an Africa-centered religion and lifestyle that started in the 1930s based on his teachings as well as the Abrahamic covenant in the Bible. One of Garvey's most famous sayings was, "Look to Africa where a Black king shall be crowned, he shall be the Redeemer" (Dagnini 2009). The king who Garvey was referring to was Ethiopian Emperor Haile Selassie I. Despite Selassie not seeing himself as God, many Rastafarians believed he was a biblically-sanctioned savior and perhaps even the second coming of Jesus Christ. Furthermore, in the Bible it is stated that Jesus will return as the Lion of Judah (New

Living Translation, Rev. 5:5), and this is why Rastafarians wore dreadlocks: "to symbolize a lion's mane and the return of a powerful leader" (Dagnini 2009). The late Bob Marley introduced the hairstyle into mainstream culture in the 1970s, and Whoopi Goldberg further popularized the look in the 1980s. Lauryn Hill and Lenny Kravitz proudly wore theirs in the 1990s and early 2000s (Gabbara 2016), as did famous authors like the late Toni Morrison and Alice Walker. The new natural hair movement has also helped the resurgence of locs in recent years, with popular figures such as Ava Duvernay, Ledisi, Willow and Jaden Smith, Chloe x Halle, and The Weeknd all making locs part of their signature look (Gabbara 2016).

There is also a website called Dear Locs, which is specifically dedicated to the loc'd community. Dear Locs focuses on the loc'd men and women influencers such as Keisha Charmaine, Thorton Paul, and Linea (AKA Locs of Poetry), to name just a few. Unfortunately, though, the loc'd community and locs-care are often still overlooked within the natural hair community and natural hair care industry.

Jocarla has been on her loc'd journey for over 17 years now. For Jocarla, locs represent freedom, natural beauty, fearlessness, spiritual growth, boldness, and strength. She also states that the style is easy to maintain, style, and care for. She loves her locs and is proud to wear them as her CROWN: she wouldn't want it any other way.

Within the natural hair movement, there are natural hair meet-up events where those with natural hair come together and celebrate being natural. What makes these events cool is that visitors get to see fellow Black women and girls fiercely and boldly embracing their tresses. A natural hair event becomes even more magical with all the variations of "Sis, your hair is so beautiful" or "Girl, you better work that hair." Visitors and attendees will feel awe seeing the wide variety of hair textures and styles. Then there is often that moment when you can meet your hair twin (a person who shares the same hair type as you), and you both become overwhelmed with joy. To add the icing on top of the cake, your favorite YouTube "Naturalista" can be a keynote speaker at the event. Many of such event's agendas consist of introductions to the keynote and guest speakers, discussions about caring for and loving natural hair, and sessions about having confidence in natural hair and yourself. Oftentimes there is also a question and answer (Q&A) period when anyone can stand up and ask her questions. Depending on the topics being discussed, conversations can become profound to the point where there is not a dry eye in the room.

    These events can be a place of healing based on attendees sharing their natural hair stories, and even when controversies or heated discussions occur, the master of ceremonies (MC) can use humor and an appeal to everyone's shared experience to defuse the tension. Attendees also jam out to tunes from DJs who provide entertainment for the event. Along with the event, hosts also often have goodie bags of hair products for attendees and prizes for the first five to ten who purchased a ticket for the meet-up.

Over the years, natural hair events have expanded to include meetings about entrepreneurship, financial literacy, health and fitness, mental health, and more. These events have also become a place where small businesses can showcase their hair products, books, jewelry, skin care, and make-up, among others. These natural hair events are accessible on platforms like Meetup Group or by googling terms such as "natural hair events near me."

UNRAVELING THE STORY OF BLACK/AFRICAN HAIR

Jade's Hair Story

My name is Jade A. and I was born and raised in Washington, D.C. As far as my cultural background goes I am Black, but unfortunately, not much else is known about my family history. In my free time I like to read and also just create. I love writing, painting, photography, and basically any outlet that allows me to express myself.

Growing up, I had positive views about my hair thanks to my parents. I know most people reacted to me in a positive

The Natural Hair Movement of the 21st Century

way because my hair texture was not what people would call "nappy." I can remember that people always seemed to be saying "oh they have good hair" to me and my sisters. We all had different hair types and textures, but I don't think I ever felt I had negative feelings about my hair as a child, even though two of my sisters had a looser curl pattern. I had my hair pressed a few times growing up for special occasions and during high school I got my first perm. I decided to return to natural right before the start of my sophomore year of college. As an adult I still love my hair and I am in awe of what it can do. I have struggled with returning natural because my hair texture is completely different now due to hormones and other factors. It has been a process of re-learning things about my hair and how to keep it healthy and styled.

As for the natural hair movement, I think it is a combination of being a trend but also an act of resistance and self-love. There are natural hair bloggers and vloggers, thousands of products to choose from, and so much more information out in the world about our hair, and many people have taken advantage of this "trend." It has also become an act of resistance and for Black women to be proud of wearing their natural hair, especially when so often it is still deemed as unprofessional or we are banned from wearing certain hairstyles in the workplace. I think this movement has helped to shed a light on how damaging Eurocentric beauty standards are and also helped Black women to embrace their own beauty, whether they are rocking natural hair, weave, perm, braids, locs, or wigs.

Ebony's Hair Story

My name is Ebony and I was born in Montserrat in the

The Natural Hair Movement of the 21st Century

West Indies. I came to the U.S. when I was 2 years old. My father is from St. Vincent, so I am part Vincentian. My hobbies include watching comedies, laughing, gardening, hanging out with friends and family, and dining out.

I am a Gen X-er. This generation was concerned about hair being straight and processed from the 80s through the 2000s. It wasn't until recently that people started embracing their natural hair. I had my hair pressed for most of my younger years and then relaxed during my teen and young adult years. During the time my hair was relaxed, my edges would routinely thin, whether from stress or whatever the other factors may have been. I went natural in my mid to late 20s for several years, then returned to a relaxer for a year or two. During that time, my hair thinned at the edges again and that helped me decide to go back to natural hair. I started with locs the first time, and then the second time, with faux locs that I wore until my hair achieved the length I preferred.

I love having locs and find so much versatility in wearing them. However, as an adult, I still struggle with hair loss near the edges and at my crown. I'm not sure why, but I think I have to pay more attention to washing and moisturizing my hair more frequently. Although I have my hair struggles on occasion, I feel empowered to have my hair natural and am so proud that other sisters are embracing theirs as well.

As a small youth, I was very much aware that children who had long, relaxed, and/or wavy hair were treated more favorably by adults than those of us who had more tightly coiled or "nappy" hair. Those who were light-skinned were treated even more favorably. Those of us with tightly coiled hair did not have many role models on TV or magazines and were not led to feel beautiful. I often struggled with that myself. Since then, though, I've embraced my beauty and tried to get my daughter to embrace hers as well. My daughter struggles with embracing her inner beauty and this is probably attributed to what is available to young people on social media. My hope is that she is able to embrace and love the skin she's in.

Chapter 4

Conflicting Sides of the Natural Hair Movement

From the outside, the natural hair movement may appear idyllic: like fluffy clouds of shea butter and gum drops infused with coconut oil. The reality, though, is that the movement can be contradicting. For instance, there is always talk about embracing your natural hair and getting away from the "creamy crack" (a term sometimes used to describe relaxers or perms), but there are also issues within the same community about certain natural features being valued more highly than others. Texturism, for example, means discrimination against someone based on their hair texture or hair type. It usually involves the glorification of an individual's straight or loosely curled, coiled, or waved natural hair texture over another's kinkier or tightly coiled natural hair texture (A'Cylo 2019). In the case of colorism, this is discrimination by which Black or People of color (POC) of a lighter hue are treated better or given preferable treatment as opposed to Black or POC with darker skin (Reece 2018).

To go even further, there is also featurism, which essentially is based on society accepting or preferring certain types of features over other types (Hernandez, 2018). All three biases—colorism, texturism, and featurism—stem from how historically, European features have been the standard of beauty rather than African features (Hernandez, 2018). Most African people and people of African descent typically have broader noses and fuller lips, while most Europeans and people of European descent typically have narrower noses and thinner lips. On the other hand, there are African people and people of African descent who have narrower noses or thinner lips.

And yet, if Africans are the most genetically diverse

group in the world (Achenbach 2009), why is it strange to see Africans or people of African descent with a wide variety of features, shades, and hair textures? This diversity of hues, facial appearance, and hair types is also due to the effects of chattel slavery, colonialism, and inter-racial marriages (though that is a subject that could fill another entire book). The main thing to recognize here is that colorism, texturism, and featurism are related, but people can feel their effects differently. For example, there are Black women with darker skin who can experience colorism while also benefitting from texturism and featurism. Remarks such as "white girl dipped in chocolate" or "she's dark but has good hair" often validate the issues of colorism, texturism, and featurism (A'Cylo, 2019). Meanwhile, although light skinned Black women may benefit from colorism, they can experience texturism and featurism, hearing comments such as "she is a waste of light skin" because they may not have the "looser curl" pattern or Eurocentric features (A'Cylo, 2019).

In the natural hair community, there have been cases where influencers with looser curl or wave patterns, or type 2-3 hair, received more praise and higher traffic on their social media pages as opposed to influencers with tighter curls, waves, or type 4 hair. This can be seen by something as seemingly simple as the number of likes and positive comments on a social media post. In 2015, Yasmin Harrell conducted a study called "The Development of Microaggressions in the Online Natural Hair Community: A Thematic Analysis" as part of her master's thesis at Georgia State University; her work explored micro-aggressions in the online natural hair community. Harrell's research did in fact point out texturism throughout the natural hair community. A way in which she found this happening was that women with looser curl patterns were more likely to receive positive comments and likes on social media, compared with those who have kinkier hair (Greaves, 2019). The study explored popular blogs and sites such as Curly Nikki and Black Girl Long Hair, along with YouTube vlog influencers like Jouelzy and Taren Guy. Harrell found that YouTube influencers Jouelzy and Taren Guy implied that these "Good Hair" and "Bad Hair" ideas occurred as a result of long, type-3 curls being viewed as "more desirable," since this texture is overrepresented in natural hair care product marketing (Harrell, 2015).

4c natural hair YouTube influencer Chizi Duru has indicated the findings of Harrell's study directly. Duru states that Harrell's research hits the nail in the head when two different hair types are subjected to comparison. Duru explains that she usually receives positive comments from her audience on her own page. However, when her photo is reposted to a general natural hair page on Instagram, where all curly textures are showcased, texturism is displayed to the highest degree (reported by Greaves 2019). Instagram users have called her hair "nappy," which is an offensive and degrading term to describe type 4 or kinky/coily hair, while others have commented on her hair looking dry (reported by Greaves 2019). To correct those who made references to Duru's hair being dry, type-4 hair or kinky hair generally gets dry. Duru also observed that those with looser, type 3 hair featured on the same platforms are praised. "It's so crazy to see the contrast," she says, adding that these cold sentiments "mainly come from other Black people" (reported by Greaves 2019).

UNRAVELING THE STORY OF BLACK/AFRICAN HAIR

A few years back there was a meme of several ladies with type 2 and 3 hair, as well as two ladies with type 4 hair. The meme stated, "Some of y'all with a [degrading term] don't know the difference." The women with type 4 texture had their hair labeled as nappy, while on the other hand, the women with type 2 and 3 texture hair were called natural. This meme displayed texturism, colorism, and featurism, as well as misogyny. What the anonymous creator of this meme failed to realize is that both of the hair textures are natural hair. However, that whole meme displayed and depended on negative depictions of kinkier hair.

These types of insensitive memes influenced naturalista jaynellenicole to launch her platform. When interviewed, jaynellenicle has said that "I wanted to show other people that 4C hair can look just as beautiful [as looser curls], we can do just as many styles, and our hair is just as versatile" (reported by Greaves 2019). In 2002-2011 when women started to return natural, they began using YouTube to capture their journeys, but it was hard to find an influencer with type 4 hair, especially 4c hair. However, influencers like Jenelle

B. Stewart (KinkyCurlyCoilyMe), Jouelzy, Natasha Gaspard (Mane Moves), Trudy Susan (4Chairchick), and Laila Jean (Neffyfrofro/Fusion of cultures), gave Black women and girls with 4C hair hope through their natural hair channels. These YouTubers documented their 4C hair journeys and showed the many ways it could be styled, telling viewers not to think of their hair as a limitation.

A related issue is that when most type 4 ladies reach shoulder- to waist-length hair, it's only then that they mostly receive admiration or more followers. YouTube influencer Kilahmazing, who has been natural since 2013, saw a tweet of a lady with long 4C hair and a caption stating "They don't appreciate 4c hair until its long." Kilahmazing agreed, based on how some natural hair companies only showcased medium to long hair, but not much shorter hair – and especially not short 4c hair.

Another YouTube influencer, Joynavon, returned natural in 2011. In the beginning of her natural hair journey, she explained that she didn't see many YouTubers with the same hair type as her. One day, she created her first natural hair video and many commentators stated how amazing it was to finally see someone with hair like theirs. Even so, it wasn't until 2016 that Joynavon really began taking her natural hair vlogging seriously. She began working with natural hair brands, and, like many YouTube influencers, would use the products and do a hair tutorial video along with her review. However, it came to the point that when Joynavon would make content, there were some brands that didn't share her videos on their pages. As she looked into this, Joynavon observed that some of the companies were only posting videos of women with natural hair that was longer and had looser curl patterns, but not as many with short kinky/coily hair. Joynayon also mentioned that women with darker skin weren't even represented in many cases. As a result of these kinds of experience, she became very selective of the hair care brands she worked with because she believes that representation matters. She also wants people in the natural hair community to move away the notion that short hair is unhealthy simply because it is not long. She wants to raise awareness that people can choose to have short hair just because they prefer that particular length and not because they can't achieve long hair. She affirms that "Since I appreciate my short 4c hair or because my hair is short, I don't want to be boxed out of different avenues" (Joynavon 2019). She also expresses the idea that while she is happy for those with long or looser curl patterns and how they are able to find platforms and inspiration easily, she also wishes that women with short kinky hair can have the same exposure as well. She has said that "I also understand that people can obsess with long hair irrespective to your hair type; however type 4 hair isn't well received during the big chop, TWA, and awkward stage (Hair that is longer than a teeny weeny afro and too short to put in a bun) of the natural hair journey" (Joynavon 2019).

    Members of the Black community as a whole should take responsibility to start embracing and celebrating all textures, rather than pitting one curl type against another. A way that we can break the cycle, according to Duru, is for Black people to start being more mindful of the type of language they associate with 4C hair. Using words like "unmanageable," "bad," "knotty," "rough," and "tough" all have a negative connotation, she notes: "They just ooze negativity, and I don't appreciate it" (reported by Greaves 2019). She encourages replacing those types of words to describe 4C hair with more positive terms like "kinky," "coily," "beautiful," and "gorgeous," declaring that "I love my hair, and I think that we should characterize it as beautiful, defined coils" (reported by Greaves 2019). On the other hand, Anise proposes that "it's also time to start looking at traits that are unique to 4C hair, like shrinkage, as something to embrace, rather than something to try to avoid" (Greaves 2019). It is true that most Black women going natural have been bothered by hair shrinkage at some point. When you discover that your hair can transform from a cute short style to powerhouse mane, that is the distinctive part about hair shrinkage: "Shrinkage is beautiful. It's not something to be frustrated with; it is something to welcome"(Greaves 2019).

  Duru concludes that naturals of all hair types should take the time to compliment more people with 4C hair; she has put this into practice herself, revealing that "Whenever I see any young girl with this hair type, the first thing I say is, 'Your hair is so beautiful... We need to condition ourselves to think better of our hair texture" (reported by Greaves 2019).

"Natural Hair Policing" or "Natural Hair Nazism"

Although the natural hair movement is filled with great intentions such as empowerment, events to receive hair tips in order to care for your hair, or safe spaces to discuss your truth and hair story, it is a sad fact that bullying someone for not" being natural enough" has also been an issue. The terms that have been coined to describe this include natural hair "policing" or even natural hair "Nazism." The Natural Hair "Nazi" or "Police" can also be defined as a know-it-all; one who seems to think they have to be the authority on all things natural hair ("Are you a Natural Hair Nazi?"). In all honesty, the term "Natural Hair Nazi" makes me cringe because some naturals who may take natural hair to the extreme or have the belief if your hair isn't in its natural state it is not natural, stigmatizes them. Plus, the term compares people who are doing something much less objectively hateful to an actual hate group of fascists.

The point of returning natural is to deflate what the media and society presents as the standard of beauty. The natural hair movement shows that natural Black/African hair is beautiful as well. On the other hand, some naturals or even those who are not natural don't want to be shunned because they choose to wear or care for their hair in a different way.

YouTube natural hair vlogger Kimera Yvonne describes how when she first returned natural, she and other newly naturals felt compelled to follow "unheard rules" that some natural hair "Gurus" created. She rigorously followed many regimens until she realized that her hair would be fine without them. Over the course of her natural hair journey, she learned that it is all about what works for your own unique hair, plus the time and effort needed to achieve your hair goals. She explained, "I thought what everyone else was doing buying expensive products was the only thing that worked for me" (Yvonne 2017). Yvonne yearned to have taken the time to learn what worked for her hair instead of jumping on different bandwagons. She says that "I know nobody tells you to follow these rules but there are women in the natural hair community who shame you for not following what they perceive to be the right way of doing your natural hair" (Yvonne 2017). From her experience, a few individuals will criticize you for doing something different than what the community suggests. This type of message defeats the purpose of the natural hair community, which is supposed to be about empowerment and self-love, and so should be a judgement-free zone. The moral of her YouTube video advocates for women going natural to do what's best for their own hair, instead of getting caught up in jumping on different trends.

Another natural hair vlogger who has noticed similar trends is Idorenyin Hope, who notes the policing that some women with natural hair enact against others. Hope has said that if you have been natural for twenty years and then decide to chemically straighten your hair, you will receive outrage from some naturals. They will even go far to say you suffer from self-hatred, Hope states. "In this case, going back to relaxing your hair seems more of a preference because you returned natural most likely to achieve healthy hair or have the experience of your natural hair. Throughout your natural hair journey you learned about your hair and accepted what it does. Moreover, you took the time out to embrace your natural hair and had spent time with it and now you reached a point where you want to relax your hair for a change" (Hope 2018).

    Hope also points out if you dye your hair a different color from its natural color, some members of the community will say that your hair is no longer natural. Furthermore, Hope spoke out about being bashed for the choice to use products that aren't 100% organic. For instance, one of the "natural hair rules" has been that if the products have ingredients that you cannot pronounce, then those products are bad for your hair. The reality, Hope says, is that it's better to, say, look up those ingredients or be aware of the chemicals in the products and actually research whether they are bad for your hair or not. An ironic thing about the natural hair police, Hope says, is that "they forget that they all had their hair relaxed at some point, like most of us in the natural hair community. Hope asserts that many of them may have had biases toward natural hair prior to returning natural. At the end of Hopes video, she addresses "why do some naturals take to heart what another natural does with their hair?" (Hope 2018). The key here is to have hair that is in good health.

In another case, for the past decade there have been taboos against using hair grease in the natural hair community. Some of the old wives' tales have been that hair grease dries out your hair, clogs your scalp pores and hair follicles, and stops growth retention. Interestingly, back in the day hair grease was a hair care staple in many Black households and many people had full heads of hair while using hair grease. The prime ingredients in hair grease are petroleum and mineral oil. Though petroleum, also known as crude oil or petrolatum, is a fossil fuel, when it is properly refined, it has no known health concerns and can found in many personal care products (Japour 1939). Mineral oil, on the other hand, is a highly purified, lightweight ingredient. Like petroleum, when it has been refined, mineral oil is used in baby lotions, cold creams, ointments, and many other cosmetic and personal care products, due to its ability to help reduce water loss from skin and keep it moisturized (Mineral oil 2020).

UNRAVELING THE STORY OF BLACK/AFRICAN HAIR

A few natural hair influencers have shown how hair grease isn't bad, based on how they apply it to their hair. For example, vlogger African Export was one of the earliest naturals on YouTube to counter the myth about hair grease being bad for your hair. In one of her videos she describes her favorite hair products and what works best for her 4a/b and high porosity. She talks about her hair definition not lasting and also about battling dryness. To prevent this, her hair has to have a lot of moisture (which is generally true for type 4 hair). In order to achieve a long-lasting moisturized hair style, African Export affirms that she seals her hair with petroleum-based hair products such as Blue Magic leave-in conditioner, and she uses hair grease on freshly-washed or moisturized hair. Hair grease gives her the results that she is looking for, which is sealing the moisture in her hair (and thus, becomes another version of the LOC or LCO method mentioned in the previous chapter). African Export states that the product does create build-up over time, usually after a week or two; however, by that time she is ready for a hair wash anyway. To conclude the video, she explains that she has not have any problems with hair grease, despite what is said about it in the natural hair community.

A few years later, natural hair influencer vlogger named EfikZara also testified that hair grease is not bad and addresses how this product has aided her natural hair journey. Like many other naturals, at first EfikZara didn't use grease and felt that it was detrimental to her hair. However, after some research on the ingredients and actually trying it out, EfrikZara realized that it was quite the reverse: hair grease was beneficial to her 4c hair. In one of her YouTube videos,"5 Big Lies The Natural Hair Community Lied about Grease!!", EfikZara contested the old wives' tales about hair grease, such as the idea that hair grease clogs your pores. She pointed out that cosmetic or refined petroleum (the type that is found in hair grease) is non-comedogenic, meaning that it is specifically formulated to not block pores (Sethi et al. 2016). It is mainly when you are not cleansing properly or washing your hair once you have product build up that your pores can get clogged. EfikZara also asserts that your hair has to be wet, damp, or moisturized when applying grease, in order for it to seal in the moisture.

UNRAVELING THE STORY OF BLACK/AFRICAN HAIR

This further refutes the argument about grease drying your hair: grease over dry hair will not moisturize it, unless the user also has a water-based product to go along with it. It is also said that grease can't be removed from your hair. The only way grease can be removed from hair is if you shampoo your hair regularly. The formula surfactant, most often called sodium lauryl sulfate or sodium laureth sulfate, easily removes the dirt and oil from hair (Cornwell 2017). Sulfur-based shampoo is good for removing the residue from your hair and scalp if you are using grease or a heavier hair cream. However, EfikZara also mentions other alternatives to sulfur-based shampoos, such as African Black soap, whose properties also help to cleanse hair (Lin et al 2017).

The next myth that EfikZara counters about grease is that it causes hair breakage. In actuality, she finds, grease aids length retention by being a sealant to lock the moisture in your hair (going back to the LOC or LCO method again). Using grease as a sealant prevents dryness, which is caused by lack of moisture and if untreated will eventually cause dryness. EfikZara states that Blue Magic, sulfur 8, and Doo Gro greases have all been agreeing with her hair.

The final common myth is that grease will cause breakouts on your skin. In this case, EfikZara states that it depends on the individual. According to the American Academy of Dermatology, if you have tiny bumps along your hair line, the upper part of your forehead, or around the back of your neck, then the hair care products that you are using may be the reason. Some shampoos, conditioners, and styling products can cause whiteheads, and the medical term for products causing acne is "acne cosmetic." One of the best ways to avoid acne cosmetic is by researching the labels on your hair and skin products. The key is to look for labels that won't clog your pores, oil free, non-comedogenic, and non-acnegenic (Fulton 2001). It is still harmful to assume that hair grease will always cause this effect for all users.

In order to help halt the "policing" of how someone cares for their natural hair, there has to be a dialogue backed with research and not just experiences of which hair care method is better than another. Just because one woman had success with a particular product doesn't mean that it will be the same for someone else, and vice versa. Instead of policing, a better way to increase awareness about natural hair, hair care, and hair care products is to encourage others to investigate the ingredients inside the products they use or want to try, and to determine whether they are good or not. Partaking in this kind of action instead of simply judging would reduce the number of Black women and girls feeling condemned for choosing to use a particular product, or for doing their hair in a particular way of their own choice.

Jessica's Hair Story

Hello! My name is Jessica, and I am a first-generation

Conflicting Sides of the Natural Hair Movement

Haitian American woman from upstate NY. I've traveled a lot, both in pursuit of my career and then just for fun! My husband and I have a YouTube channel and an Instagram page called @dariusdestinations where we document our travels, life, and even feature our 3-year-old son. We started doing video blogs for our son so that he had a bank of memories of his parent's lives prior to his arrival into this world and also during his childhood. Additionally, my husband and I have been working on a podcast called @deardadpodcast to highlight the importance of fathers in their children's lives and its effects on children overall, while simultaneously spotlighting and recognizing those who are positive examples of what being a dad is all about!

While creating video blogs, vacationing, or even while working professionally, one thing that ALWAYS seems to come up is my hair. Everywhere I go, someone comments on or compliments my hair. It is flattering today, but my journey was not always so smooth. Looking back at childhood pictures and photo albums, I notice my hair was always well-kept, long and healthy, and natural. But by the time I reached ten years old, my hair was straightened with a relaxer for the first time. At ten, I barely knew who I was as a person, but one thing I did know is that I needed and wanted to assimilate into the predominantly white environment that I grew up in. While my hair looked amazing straight, I started to grow frustrated with the amount of shedding I experienced with the relaxers. My previously thick, coily mane was becoming thin and straight, resembling water from a drinking fountain. And the transition periods between relaxer touch-ups were hideous! By the time I was a teenager, I found myself gravitating to the neo-soul music movement, which helped me rediscover my roots (no pun intended), and my soul as a Black woman in a predominantly white area. Consequently, by my senior year in high school in 2002 (yes, I'm an old head, lol), I started finding inspiration in artists like Eryka Badu, Musiq Soulchild, Floetry, Kindred Family Soul, India Arie, Leyla James, and movies like *Love Jones, The Wood*, and even *Bring It On*, plus so much more! They all inspired me to start rocking headwraps, and most importantly, sparked the idea of returning to my natural hair. It was like finding a missing piece of myself that was hiding in plain sight, right on my head and in my heart.

Let's rewind a bit, though. So I started off by saying that I am a first-generation Haitian American, so for my family, the thought of deviating from "social norms" with relation to hair was NOT what my family wanted to hear at that time. I was told that I would never get married if I stop relaxing my hair, and that I would never get a job if I returned to my natural hair. I was told to go natural only after I had snatched and locked down a husband—the list goes on! It was so confusing for me as a teenager because the relaxer really thinned my hair, and I didn't feel like myself when I was wearing it. Every month when I noticed the new growth coming in, it was full of life, strength, thickness, and health, and it put me in a very conflicting position when reapplying the harsh chemicals on my roots to achieve a look that did not make me feel like my truest self. So when I went away to college at Northeastern University in Boston, which was about 4 hours away from my home in New York, I finally decided that this was my chance to stop relaxing my hair. This was my chance to find me. So I did just that.

UNRAVELING THE STORY OF BLACK/AFRICAN HAIR

Over time, the new growth came in; I trimmed about an inch or two off my ends and then got braid extensions to disguise the awkward transition phase when letting the relaxed ends grow out. I did this all throughout undergrad, and when I went home for the holidays, I'd get fresh new braid extensions or a press and curl. Until Christmas 2005, when I showed up to my home with a full, lustrous afro! I walked into my home with such pride and poise because I felt like me, my truest version of me! But when I noticed my mother's facial expression, I quickly felt myself recoiling to feeling so small. I will never forget that moment. She. Was. Pissed, y'all. "How could you do this, Jessica?!", "What were you thinking?!", "Growing up, I never had hair like you, Jessica, and as my ONLY daughter, with long, beautiful hair, why would you do this TO ME!?"

This was such a defining and pivotal moment in my natural hair journey: a moment where my previous standards of beauty and the values instilled in me intersected with what I felt was right for me in navigating with who I am and what I love about being me. My family's reaction stunned me, to say the least. But one thing I knew was that I was not going to relax my hair again. Moving forward, I invited my mother to witness my journey firsthand. I asked her to hot comb my hair, which unexpectedly brought us closer and allowed her to see the beauty in natural hair up close and personal. Those moments of her hot combing my hair was a healthy compromise where I'd have my hair straight like she wanted, but on my terms and her act of her physically hot combing my hair allowed her to see the benefits of returning natural. She saw my hair transformation go back to a healthy state. She saw the length, strength, and rebirth of my hair. Witnessing the versatility in my natural hairstyles, like pineapple updo's, bantu knot twist outs, braid outs, protective two hand twists undo's, truly inspired her! And this eventually converted her and all the critics I faced during my journey to embark on their own natural hair journeys.

    Today, in 2020, I personally do not think I know anyone with a relaxer anymore. Throughout adulthood, I've definitely explored all the amazing things I could do with my hair. My hair gave me a sense of self-worth, self-confidence, reassurance, and a sense of pride. In fact, my natural hair journey led me to finally loc my hair in 2013. I appreciated and valued my natural hair journey so much that I decided that I didn't want to shed any part of it anymore. To me, locing my hair is a commitment I've made to my hair: to hold on to each and every coil, curl, strand, and nap. Almost as if I'm hoarding my own hair, lol!

All jokes aside, I feel as though each retwist/retightening session is like an initiation for my new growth to join into its own loc community. It's such an amazingly freeing process. Seeing the increased popularity of natural hair and locs in society took me by surprise initially because it made me recall all the backlash and ignorant "advice" that I received from so many people when the styles were not as popular. I remember feeling a little bitter knowing that I took the time and journey to get my hair where it was while facing so much criticism along the way, while it seemed like everyone else could just buy the afro or get loc extensions, goddess locs, etc., and be totally celebrated for it. I'll be honest, it stung a little. Especially when those I received the most criticism from seemed to "jump on the bandwagon" afterward as if they were not public enemy number 1 to me just a few years prior. But then I realized that the critics were possibly negatively conditioned to think the way they did, say the things they said, and believe the things they were taught to believe in the name of tradition and social norms that exclude highlighting diversity in relation to natural hair. And at one point, my beliefs had aligned with theirs. So having the opportunity to illustrate versatility and diversity in hair allows me to be able to help rewrite their narrative of what natural hair is and how it shapes who we are as Black women. Recognizing and accepting that everyone's journey is unique to them, allowed me to encourage others to embrace and love themselves for who they are.

Now that others are deciding to embark on their own natural hair journeys to help themselves rediscover and re-love themselves, I find myself gladly supporting the movement. The ability to turn my brief moment of bitterness into long-term advocacy for natural hair, in turn helped me grow as a person too by reshaping my way of thinking. Now that I know how being a role model for positivity, self-love, and self-discovery may have its backlash and obstacles, I must remember that the end game is greater than the grueling process. Being a positive influence will impact others in a positive way. Loving myself for me, finding a sense of pride in my natural beauty not only lifts me up, but also inspires others around me. That is what my natural hair journey has taught me. And I am so happy I went along for the ride!

Oju's Hair Story

Hi! I am Oju and I am originally from Monrovia, Liberia. I immigrated to the States as a child in 1985 and grew up in North Carolina. I am a Gen Xer. Growing up as a Gen X-er, the way I viewed my hair was shaped by the styles of the day and what I saw my cousins, mom, aunties, and other girls and women wearing and mimicking. Back home as a girl in Liberia, I wore my hair naturally, most often donning neat cornrows or pig tails ornamented with colorful, thick yarn ribbons. It's all I knew to wear and love until I moved to America.

Generally speaking, the jheri curl and relaxed or pressed hair were the two main standards I saw when I came to the States. Since my hair was not naturally either of those two textures, I subconsciously became more and more dissatisfied with my own hair. My mom never allowed me to get a jheri curl, but my hair was relaxed before middle school. Before relaxers, my hair was pressed.

I am currently relaxer-free as of April 2017 and will never turn back. As an adult, I now celebrate every part of me that God created, including my tight coils. I am still learning about my fully natural hair. I most often wear protective styles because of my busy and active lifestyle, so washing and styling

UNRAVELING THE STORY OF BLACK/AFRICAN HAIR

my hair is always an adventure...even when my style goal is not a success. For a long time I saw the natural hair movement as a trend and a bandwagon that I refused to jump on. Today, though, I recognize it as an acceptance and love of self for Black women AND men. But I also hope that acceptance of our natural hair fuels and gives confidence in and validation for the beauty unique to our remarkable and diverse genetics...beauty often imitated but never fully duplicated.

Chapter 5

Inclusivity within the Natural Hair Movement

There have been many exchanges and debates about the natural hair community opening its doors to other curly-haired individuals of different racial and ethnic backgrounds. The natural hair movement was started by Black women (African and of African descent). However, most of the people who are a part of this community identify as Black, POC, Latinx, or multi-racial.

This is a sensitive topic because, historically, Afro-textured hair was not perceived as beautiful. Within the natural hair community, a space has been made for Afro-textured hair to shine and be uplifted. However, with the way that the movement of the 21st century has expanded, it is understandable for other POC and even non-POC with curly hair to be interested in learning to wear and celebrate their natural hair as well. On the other hand, newcomers to the movement must be aware that many Black women and girls, at some point in their lives, have chemically straightened their natural hair because it was deemed as "unmanageable" or "ugly." The point of the natural hair movement was to reject appeasing society's standards of hair and beauty, which are very different for Black women and women of color than for many others.

    A couple years ago, the founder and CEO of Shea Moisture, Mr. Richelieu Dennis, received backlash after the creation of a new ad and marketing campaign, called #EverybodyGetsLove. This ad, a one-minute snippet produced by Vayner Media, featured a series of women stating how Shea Moisture products freed them from "hair hate." Although the brand is known for uplifting and featuring Black women with curly, kinky, and coily hair types as its target audience, many were taken by surprise with the ad, which featured four women—only one of whom was Black (reported by Payne and Duster 2017). Several Black women were baffled and took to social media to call the #AllHairMatters campaign an elimination of the loyal demographic who had supported the brand from the beginning. Responses like this one, from Twitter user @thetrudz, were common: "Shea Moisture been drew a line in the sand, but now they're throwing the sand in the eyes of dark BW (Black Women) w/ kinky hair" (reported by Payne and Duster 2017).

Due to the backlash, Shea Moisture pulled this ad from Facebook, writing "Wow, okay – so guys listen, we really messed this one up." Considering the discrimination that Black women often face in respect to hair and beauty standards, a number of white supporters on social media were expressed as white washing, a marketing ploy, and a rejection of Black women. Dennis responded that, "This was not our intent. And I understand how that feels to them," and in addition, states that "while the campaign is heavily representative of women of color, we didn't explain to the community what the larger campaign is about, which is about women's hair challenges" (reported by Payne and Duster 2017). Dennis went on to mention that they filmed and interviewed over 40 women of different ethnicities and hair types in an effort to share that Shea Moisture has solutions for all. He is also aware that some women feel that Shea Moisture will abandon them to a larger audience. However, he stated, that is not the case: Shea Moisture has been acclaimed for its use of natural, ethically-sourced organic ingredients. The company was more of "a mission with a business, rather than a business with a mission, Dennis explains" (reported by Payne and Duster 2017).

On the other hand, it should be considered that the natural hair care world is very competitive now, compared to when the product was first launched. Dennis also added that the business has to grow, claiming that "Brands that didn't serve Women of Color (WOC) for decades are all of the sudden creating campaigns for them to go after because of the growth they've seen coming from us. The competition that we now see puts business like ours at risk" (reported by Payne and Duster

2017). A twitter user named @OkiaSpeaks expressed her full support of the company's expansion via Twitter: "I really don't get why y'all are mad at Shea Moisture. Y'all should want Black business to start getting this white coin as well" (reported by Payne and Duster 2017). The issue, however, is not about Shea Moisture's expansion; what it *is* about is continuing to represent the Black audience who helped fuel the company's growth in the first place.

To further investigate the topic of inclusivity, founder Antonia Opiah and other colleagues of Un-ruly created a platform called "Black hair is…" This initiative was a debate involving twelve women, six with relaxed hair and another six with natural hair. The discussion studies what Black hair should be and what it really is, based on wedges within the community. This campaign is about embracing the possibilities of our hair and praising its versatility, despite any one's individual hair choices. The goal is to create an environment that allows a balance of differences and choices. Un-ruly has partnered up with Smooth 'N Shine Hair Company to bring its campaign to life.

UNRAVELING THE STORY OF BLACK/AFRICAN HAIR

In a YouTube episode of "Black hair is…", one topic was "Can white women be in the natural hair movement?" A total of six women were a part of the discussion, which was split down the middle: three answered yes, and the other three disagreed. To point out in the interview, three ladies had loose natural hair ranging from 3-4c hair while the other three had their hair in protective styles such as box braids, buns, and puffs. All six participants gave valid reasons on why or why not white women should be included in the natural hair movement. They also opened doors where there is hope for a healthy discussion about inclusivity in the natural hair community, along with having a space in which to not feel ashamed for not wanting to do so.

This is hardly the only question at hand, though. Black parents and caregivers know the amount of time and work it takes to keep our hair healthy and maintained, along with doing so for our children. However, imagine white or non-Black parents or caregivers who have Black or multiracial children? Black and multi-racial children's hair texture mainly falls in the category of type 3 and type 4. Non-Black parents or caregivers will have questions about caring for their curly, wavy, kinky, or coily haired children. Parents or caregivers will also need avenues to help their children to embrace their natural hair. This leaves an invitation for them into the natural hair community.

When Rory Mullen first adopted her African American baby at 6 days old, she didn't take too much notice of her hair care. Mullen, who is white, has stated that, "I was a motorcycle riding tomboy who wore nothing but ponytails underneath my helmet, so caring for my own hair was something I never did" (reported by Varma-White 2014). However, after her daughter Boo (a family nickname) arrived with a full head of hair, Mullen realized that she was going to need help caring for it. While looking for tips on the care of Boo's hair, Mullen observed that there were mostly blogs for adult hair care and products, and there weren't many geared toward younger kids. So in 2010, when Boo was 2, Mullen started the blog Chocolate Hair/Vanilla Care, to chronicle the mother-daughter journey of Boo's haircare (reported by Varma-White 2014). Throughout the start of her blog, many of her audience were mostly other trans-racial adoptive parents. Mullen states, "So many times adoptive parents want to know what 'miracle product' will 'fix' their child's hair" (reported by Varma-White 2014). She also revealed, "They are usually disappointed with my answer. First of all, there's nothing about the hair that needs to be 'fixed' or 'tamed' or 'controlled'—the thing that needs to be addressed is the understanding of the unique requirements of natural hair" (reported by Varma-White 2014). Over the course of four years Mullen encapsulated her daughter's natural hair journey as she learned to "do hair," mostly through trial and error. The Chocolate Hair/Vanilla Care blog displayed Boo's various hairstyles, including cornrows, Bantu knots, twist-outs, and flat twist up-dos. Mullen's blog title was inspired by a book she had read while preparing to adopt, Marguerite A. Wright's *I'm Chocolate, You're Vanilla: Raising Healthy Black and Biracial Children in a Race-Conscious World.*

Another white mother, Megan Wiigs, was inspired to start "Hair-raising Adventures," which is based off the hair care of her bi-racial daughter, after reading blogs such as Mullen's. Mrs. Wiggs states that, being a fan of big curly hair, she loved her daughter's growing fro and would leave it out often. Being from an ethnically diverse neighborhood she would receive compliments on her daughter's hair. In other instances, though, others "would look at her hair, shift their gaze from her hair to me, and then quickly look away. I began to see a pattern in terms of these opposite reactions. In general, people who were not Black loved her big hair and went out of their way to tell me so. People who were Black looked away" (reported by Varma-White 2014). In the beginning, Wiggs didn't pay much attention to this, until her in-laws would insist on doing her daughter's hair, and Wiigs was always surprised by how good it looked after being well-vaselined and coaxed into twists and braids (reported by Varma-White 2014). Once, Wiggs' friend who is Black warned her that if she continued to leave JJ's hair loose, "it would get more and more knotty, break, and possibly even lock" (reported by Varma-White 2014). She realized that she needed to learn techniques of caring for JJ's hair, including doing protective styles like natural braids and twists. Eventually the blog "Hair-raising adventures" included not just white moms, but also lots of Black moms, some of whom Wiggs reports "didn't have a lot of experience with natural hair because they had been relaxing their hair since they were children themselves" (reported by Varma-White 2014). Although Wiggs no longer updates her site, she says she will always cherish the education about hair and the friendship she got from other moms via blogging.

    Mullen of Chocolate Hair / Vanilla Care says that Boo " is knowledgeable in styles and haircare such as the personal responsibility she must undertake when wearing her curls free" (reported by Varma-White 2014). She will often give Mullen drawings of what she wants her hair to look. Some of her favorite styles are done in shapes and characters, such as hearts and shamrocks or Hello Kitty and Mickey Mouse. Boo's hair is normally styled once a week; however, she also wears protective styles that can last a month or two (reported by Varma-White 2014). Mullen states, "What I love most is [that] my daughter appreciates her hair and has never thought of it as a burden. Whereas some people feel that sitting for long hours to do hair would be unreasonable for a child, her perspective is quite the opposite. She doesn't understand how some girls have to do their hair every day. That's just crazy to her" (reported by Varma-White 2014).

In 2014, Mullen curated the very basic styling posts that she had written into a beginning hairstyling book called *Chocolate Hair Vanilla Care: A Parent's Guide to Beginning Natural Hair Styling*. She also retired her blog because natural hair resources for parents online had broadened in scope and contributors, and Mullen felt it was time to step back and let those who have natural hair take their rightful place as teachers. She is thankful for the love and support of the many naturalistas, bloggers, and entrepreneurs she met along the way. Today, Mullen continues to raise her daughter along with writing novels and making crafty things.

Tamekia Swint, a Black stylist, has also opened the door for broader inclusivity in the natural hair community. Swint is the founder and director of Styles 4 Kidz (originally Styles 4 Girlz), a non-profit organization based in Chicago that helps transracial families care for and style their kids' hair. Whether parents have adopted kids with natural kinky or coily hair, or have given birth to multi-racial children, this organization helps bring families together through hair! Styles 4 Kidz's mission is to provide high-quality, compassionate hair care education and services for kids with textured hair in foster care, transracial adoptive families, or biracial families. The organization's vision is to build a diverse community of people creating and celebrating hairstyles that boost kids' self-esteem and cultural pride.

Styles For Girlz, the organization's original name, was founded in 2010 after Swint taught a hair braiding class on a Missions Trip to Poland to a group of students at an English Language Learning (ELL) camp. Upon her arrival back to the United States, she was introduced to a transracial adoptive mom who was in need of affordable hair care for her three daughters. Delighted with Swint's work, Mary referred her to a group of adoptive parents who were also in need of hair care services for their little ones along with a safe place to learn how to properly care for their transracial and multi-racial children's hair without being ridiculed and criticized. Swint thus learned that there was a need for Styles For Girlz not only with Mary and her friends, but also among multiracial families

Inclusivity within the Natural Hair Movement

and transracial foster and adoptive families throughout Illinois. The organization grew from serving just 3 clients in 2010 to over a thousand clients throughout the United States in 2020. Beginning in 2013, Styles For Girlz expanded its mission to provide in-home hair care education, training, and services to children in foster care, children residing in residential facilities and detention centers, and special needs children with textured hair. In addition, the organization changed its name from Styles For Girlz to Styles 4 Kidz (S4K) in 2016. Eight years later, S4K opened one of the first nonprofit—501(c)(3) tax-exempt—salons of its kind, where multiracial foster and adoptive kids are empowered to embrace their natural, ethnic crown. To quote the organization's mission statement, it's all about "Hair Care With Heart."In respect to inclusivity in the natural hair community—or the Black/African hair community as a whole—cultural appropriation ties into this debate as well. According to Bruce Ziff and Pratima Roa, law professors and the authors of *Borrowed Power: Essays on Cultural Appropriation*, this term describes " the taking from a culture that is not one's own of intellectual property, cultural expression or artifacts, history and ways of knowledge" (Ziff & Rao 2010, as cited in Grays 2016). These authors also state that appropriation occurs when a privileged group—that is, a group that has economic, political, and institutional power—borrows or steals from an oppressed or marginalized group, without compensation or acknowledgement and often putting the stolen idea(s) to some different use than their original purpose.

Cultural appropriation can often be found regarding Black hairstyles. Braids, particularly cornrows, are a popular hairstyle among Africans and people of African descent. Cornrows, an ancient style, are widespread in Africa, where for a long time they have represented a wide range of social terrain such as religion, kinship, status, age, and ethnicity. Other forms of identity can be expressed in hairstyle (Culturally Situated Design Tools 2020). Braiding transmits cultural values between generations, expresses bonds between friends, and establishes the role of professional practitioner (Culturally Situated Design Tools 2020). This same bond of braiding hair has been preserved in many African diaspora communities as well. Throughout Africa and the diaspora, braids are not only the style that many Black girls wear growing up, but they are also a representation of who we are (Grays 2016). Given this, it isn't a surprise that some Black people feel offended when white people or non-Black POC wear braids or cornrows as a trend.

My hair in cornrow extensions. Styled by hairstylist Tee Brooklyn. Southern Divas Beauty Salon, Winston Salem, NC.

For instance, there have been some non-Black celebrities who have worn hairstyles that originated in Black/African culture but treated them as accessories and called them different styles, such as boxer braids instead of corn rows. White celebrities might also declare that these kinds of braids are "just" hairstyles, and so are available to anyone.

In the 2015 YouTube video "Don't Cash Crop my Cornrows" by feminist and Hunger Games starlet Amanda Stenberg, Stenberg called out cultural appropriation among white celebrities. Stenberg states "the issue is not wearing braids; on the other hand, the problem is the image. You have a look and style that is rooted in Black culture; however, fail to recognize the influences and see the struggles of the culture you continue to emulate" (reported by Grays 2016). She also notes that "appropriation occurs when a style leads to racist generalizations or stereotypes where it originated but deemed as high fashion, cool, or funny when the privileged take it for themselves" (reported by Grays 2016).

Fashion designer Marc Jacobs is a particular example of a white person who has experienced backlash for this: in his case, it was cultural appropriation on the runway. While debuting his Spring-Summer 2017 fashion show in 2016, the designer sparked controversy online when he sent white models down his runway with colorful faux locs. He was criticized on social media for appropriating Caribbean culture (Grays 2016). In another instance, in his Spring 2015 show, there were white models on the runway with Bantu knots, and instead of stating the actual name, they were called twisted mini-buns. Yet again Jacobs received flak for discrediting the origins of the style (Bryant, 2015). Depending on where in Africa or African diaspora community, the style is respectively named Chicken Poop Poop or Gola knots (Liberia), Chiney or China bumps (Jamaica), and Bantu knots (Southern Africa). Bantu universally translates to "people" among many African languages, and it is used to categorize over 400 ethnic groups in Africa. These knots are also referred to as Zulu knots because the Zulu people of South Africa, a Bantu ethnic group, originated the hairstyle. Sometimes the look also goes by the name of Nubian knots (Horne 2018).

UNRAVELING THE STORY OF BLACK/AFRICAN HAIR

Bantu Knots styled and worn by Tracee

To counter the backlash, Jacobs took to social media, where he stated, "All who cry 'cultural appropriation' or whatever nonsense about any race or skin color wearing their hair in any particular style or manner — funny how you don't criticize women of color for straightening their hair. I respect and am inspired by people and how they look. I don't see

Inclusivity within the Natural Hair Movement

color or race — I see people" (reported by Safronova 2016). Of course, Jacobs completely ignores how Black women and women of color are often pressured into straightening their hair, making the two examples incomparable. Other social media users pointed this out, such as Instagram user @kiidiosa stating "black women who straighten their hair were forced to conform to those standards. A form of assimilation. I'm from Canada but in America if your hair is unkept, [or] in styles such as dreads, Afros, cornrows, black women lose jobs and opportunities, and they also get ridiculed like Zendaya" (reported by Safronova 2016). This response in particular is bringing up comments that *E! News* host Giuliana Rancic made about the singer Zendaya's locs at the Oscars in 2015. @kiidiosa also asserted, "You don't see color, huh? How convenient for you. Cuz black women are reminded abt their hair and skin every day. But your privilege has allowed you that option. I loved you, also didn't take offense to the dreads, but your comment was redundant and ignorant. Shame" (reported by Safronova 2016).

    What Jacobs failed to realize is that his comments

UNRAVELING THE STORY OF BLACK/AFRICAN HAIR

overlooked the obvious reasons why women of color wear weaves or straighten their hair. Instead of starting a dialogue about the history of locs and Bantu knots, he only used the hair styles to draw attention to his clothing line to expand his own profit (Grays 2016). Historically, Black women were told their natural hair was untamed, unprofessional, or unattractive. For centuries marginalized people have conformed to standards set by dominant groups not only to get ahead but also to survive. This also ties into cultural assimilation (Grays 2016).

    We often talk about Black/African people perming their hair to look more like Caucasian hair. However, there are also people of other races who attempt to make their hair kinky or textured like that of Black people. Afro perms, along with other Black hairstyles, have been a longtime trend in Asia. For instance, "An afro perm is made by not straightening the hair, and instead, by creating hair bonds that make the hair curl. The hair stylist makes the hair into a new shape, using perming rods or rollers, and allows the new shape to develop" (reported by 1 blessed natural 2017). For a few years now, there has been a trend where there are hair YouTube tutorials by young Asian men teaching their viewers how to get an afro with straight hair. Throughout the videos they are talking about Cantu shea butter and Shea Moisture Curl Enhancing Smoothie. These are natural hair products that have been reviewed and used by Black natural hair influencers.

From one viewpoint, this could be a cross cultural mash-up, since many Black hair supply stores are run by Asian proprietors, and so hair could just be the next frontier of cultural exchange between Black and Asian communities (Tharps 2018). On the other hand, though, this can be seen as cultural appropriation. Not only are Asian men borrowing from Black hair culture, but also they're even borrowing the YouTube hair tutorial model that Black women pioneered (Tharps 2019). There is also a huge and growing trend of Asian performers, such as Kpop and Cpop groups, wearing Blackface for their debut cover art, promotional images, and music videos. Along with drawing from Black music styles like hip hop and R&B, performers such as Zico, EXO's Kai, and Bigbang's Taeyang have worn dreadlocs and braids, essentially performing Blackness for profit (Mitchell 2020).

While there have been discussions about cultural appropriation being necessary in order to preserve ancient cultural styles, this often leaves out the descendants of that culture who fight to maintain their culture themselves. Attorney Susan Scafifi, the author of *Who Owns Culture?: Appropriation and Authenticity in American Law*, has stated that cultural appropriation "can sometimes be the savior of cultural product or practice that otherwise would have faded away, like learning the history of ancient Buddhists and implementing their practices respectfully in your yoga class" (Scafidi 2005, as cited in Gray 2016). However, there is no correct way to culturally appropriate. Cultural appropriation is offensive and discredits an aspect of a culture that is not the person's own, and then makes it profitable for that person's own advantage without crediting or sharing with the culture that originated it. Thus, practices that seeks to understand and learn about another culture in an effort to broaden their perspective and connect with others cross-culturally is not about appropriating culture, but maintaining it, and so this is actually a different matter altogether.

Erin and Briel's Hair Story

My name is Erin and my daughter's name is Briel. I am from a rural town in Mingo County, West Virginia and my daughter was born in Lexington, Kentucky. My daughter and I both love to swim and go to the beach. My daughter likes baseball, bicycling, and pretty much anything active. She is a tough and brave little girl who loves to challenge herself.

I think that, when preparing for motherhood, I underestimated the efforts that would be needed to take care of my child's hair. Although I do have curly hair myself and it has been a challenge for most of my life, our situations are not the same. When I was planning for motherhood, my daughter's hair was not at the forefront of my concerns; however, I learned quickly that it would be something I needed to work on and put a lot of time and effort into.

When I was a child my mother, who has very straight and thin hair, had little idea how to care for curly hair. So I knew that when I had my own daughter, I wanted to do my absolute best to begin a hair regime as soon as possible so that she would be able to have healthy hair that she could feel confident in. So when Briel was about 18 months old, I began trying to research and find out information about how to properly care for her hair. This was a great challenge, since I had little family support to assist with this and as I did my research it seemed like many sources contradicted themselves or had different methods for different types of hair. This was all new to me at the time. Even now when she is 6 years old, I still find myself trying to research more and learning new things each day to help her. I have had a few friends who have assisted over the years, but to be honest, it has been very challenging to find help and I have done most of my research online. I find that when others do try to help, they may overlook how basic my knowledge is. Similar to how if you were teaching a child to do something for the first time, I need clear steps in full detail, as it is all so new to me.

Most of what I have learned has come from social media. Although many resources can be contradicting at times, I have found tutorials and articles online to be most useful during this journey. I would love to find more resources that give specific instructions and really simplify for those who have zero knowledge. Even on things as simple as to how to wash or condition hair or how to comb it properly. How often to wash? How often to comb out? Etc...

My daughter actually loves her natural hair. She does get discouraged at times that her hair requires so much maintenance and she will express this. I am still working on finding ways to keep it from getting into so many knots or how to appropriately care for it during sleep so that she can wear it natural more often. But it is a learning process. She does not like the maintenance because she is so young and the amount of time it takes can be frustrating to her. However, she always appears to feel confident and happy once the process over, when her hair is natural and has been cared for. My goal as a parent is to make my children feel amazing about themselves inside and out. I often felt insecure about my hair growing up and I was faced with far fewer challenges than Briel is. So I hope to teach her that natural hair is beautiful and not to be something to be insecure about. I hope to give her the tools to keep her hair healthy and to maintain it as easily as possible, so that when the time comes that she starts caring for it herself, she has the choice to fix it however she prefers and is not forced to work on repairing because of damage I created.

Chapter 6

Discrimination against Natural Hair

For over 40 years, Black workers have filed lawsuits against their places of employment due to hair discrimination. In 2010, for example, Chastity Jones was thinking of accepting a job offer from Catastrophe Management Solutions as a customer service representative. However, the offer came with one condition—she had to cut off her locs. When Jones refused, the company revoked its job offer. The company's hiring manager apparently told Jones, "They tend to get messy" (reported by Griffin 2019). On Jones's behalf, The Equal

Employment Opportunity Commission (EEOC) filed a suit in 2013, but they lost this case. Then the 11th Circuit Court of Appeals upheld the district court's ruling and dismissed the case in 2016.

Like Jones's case, many other cases against natural hair discrimination have had mixed results. Such judicial rulings, interlocked with changing social and cultural mores, have created a disputable and unclear legal situation, with courts and other governmental entities ruling on both sides of the debate. Regardless if their hair was relaxed, pressed, or natural, African Americans demanded the signing of the Civil Rights Act of 1964, which "ended segregation in public places and banned employment discrimination" (reported by Griffin 2019). The Act also created the EEOC, which operates "as the lead enforcement agency in the area of workplace discrimination" (reported by Griffin 2019). When the EEOC was founded 56 years ago, the federal government's main focus was for Black people to be granted equal access to public workplaces. However, the EEOC did not foresee that Black hair would need equal protection in the workforce as well.

Discrimination Against Natural Hair

The first recorded discrimination case against natural hair occurred in 1976 with Beverly Jeanne Jenkins v. Blue Cross Mutual Hospital Insurance. The U.S. Court of Appeals for the Seventh Circuit upheld a race discrimination lawsuit against an employer for bias against afros. Prior to the appeal, Jenkins "brought this action on her own behalf and on behalf of other persons similarly situated as a class action, charging the defendants, her former employers, with denying her promotions and better assignments, and with ultimately terminating her employment because of her "race, sex, Black styles of hair and dress," in violation of Title VII of the Civil Rights Act of 1964 (Griffin, 2019). Jenkins sought for back pay and other money damages, but on July 17, 1974, the district court denied her motion, saying that the complaint did not match the kinds that could be brought before the EEOC. Specifically, the court's explanation of not granting the class action was that:

(1) "(i)t is clear that she did not raise sex before the EEOC . . .

(2) "while there is an arguable connection to race by

the allegation of hair style discrimination, such is not sufficient to raise the panorama of alleged (racial) evils plaintiff seeks to adjudicate in her complaint"

(3) "Her class could, therefore, only be composed of those persons denied promotion or not hired for wearing an Afro hair style"; and

(4) "(n)o proof has been presented to the Court to show that this group of people would be so large that joinder of them in this action would be impracticable" (United States Court of Appeals, Seventh Circuit, 1925-1993)

Therefore, on January 21, 1975, the district court denied Jenkins her case. However, Jenkins appealed both the July 17, 1974 and January 21, 1975 orders. An appeal was made due to the fact that the trial court dismissed the complaint because of the named plaintiff's failure to qualify as representative of her class under Title VII, without giving consideration to the claim based on § 1981, and since we conclude that the relief claimed under § 1981 need not be based on any form of claim filed with the EEOC . . ." (Jenkins v. Blue Cross Mutual Hospital Insurance, Inc.). The case was remanded for the district court, as they could consider whether the plaintiff qualified as a representative of the class upon her § 1981 claim, which alleged only racial discrimination, and thereafter to consider "what equitable relief the plaintiff may be entitled to. Eventually, the district court granted hearing for Jenkins" (Jenkins v. Blue Cross Mutual Hospital Insurance, Inc.). After reviewing the case, the appeals court agreed that under Title VII of the Civil Rights Act, employees were permitted to wear afros (Griffin, 2019). However, even though afros were theoretically allowed in workplaces, the social pressure to emulate Eurocentric hair still swamped American society, impacting Black people's hair grooming choices.

In 2006, the EEOC issued its Compliance Manual on Race and Color Discrimination, which specifies guidelines around what constitutes discrimination based on physical characteristics in the workplace. The manual shields against "employment discrimination based on a person's physical characteristics associated with race, such as a person's color, hair, facial features, height and weight" (Griffin, 2019). The manual declares that, "employers can impose neatness and grooming standards, as long as racial differences are taken into account and the rules are applied equally across racial lines" (Griffin, 2019). In other words, employers cannot discriminate against an employee wearing an afro, for instance, because that is Black/African hair in its natural state. Thus, while employers might be able to request that an afro be groomed, they cannot request that it not be worn at all. Neither can they apply hairstyle rules more rigidly to hairstyles worn by Black employees. Despite this clarification from the EEOC's Compliance Manual on Race and Color Discrimination, though, there's still room for judicial interpretation, with the EEOC and federal courts disagreeing. Regarding the current debate around natural hairstyles such as locs, for instance, different parties might disagree over whether these styles constitute a racial characteristic protected by the law. Going back to the 2010 natural hair discrimination case of Jones, the Eleventh Circuit retained that the employer did not discriminate against Jones based on race because the locs hairstyle is an "alterable or changeable—characteristic" (Griffin 2019). The EEOC, on the other hand, sustained that race is a social construct that isn't strictly limited to unalterable characteristics (Griffin 2019). The Commission vows that race can also consist of "cultural characteristics related to race or ethnicity" (Griffin 2019) along with grooming practices. Sadly, the circuit court disagreed, declaring that although locs are traditionally associated with people of African descent, the company did not part take in any racial discrimination or disparaging. Although the EEOC decided not to take the case to the Supreme Court and the NAACP's subsequent request that the court hear the case was denied, other government entities have started building a foundation that tackles natural hair discrimination (Griffin 2019).

    The 1990s sitcom *Living Single* offers further examples of the debate over whether natural hairstyles like locs should be protected from natural hair discrimination in the workforce, demonstrating just how long this has been an issue in the popular consciousness. *Living Single*, which was created by Yvette Lee Bowser, aired from August 1993-January 1998. The show was based on six African American friends, four women and two men, who share their lives and love in a Brooklyn brownstone. Three of the women share an apartment, while receiving recurrent visits from a fourth buddy; then the two men who have been friends since childhood share an apartment one floor up. In a particular episode of the show, "A Hair-Razing Experience" (season 2, episode 13), writer David Wyatt sheds light on having natural hair while working in corporate America. Actor Terrance "T.C". Carson's character Kyle Barker is a successful and handsome stockbroker who wears locs and takes pride in his Black/African culture. At Barker's firm, he suggests that they take advantage of the untapped financial potential of Africa by creating a mutual fund, and he volunteers to handle the project personally. After the presentation, Barker's African American colleague and sometimes nemesis Lawrence informs him that the firm is concerned about using him as a representative, as his appearance--specifically his hair--isn't "corporate" enough. Barker does not want his career to be hindered by this, so he ponders whether he should get a haircut. He then experiences a nightmare in which he turns into a jester who submits to his bosses' every notion and is forced to dance before Maxine "Max" Shaw (played by Erika Alexander), the friend who visits the three roommates: a successful Lawyer, Shaw has a love-hate relationship with Barker for several seasons before they eventually become a couple. When Barker goes back to work, he calls a meeting that he attends wearing a suit with a vest made from African mud cloth, which reflects his cultural identity. During the meeting, Barker expressed his sense that when he joined the firm, advancement was based on each incoming employee's abilities. He also says that it seems as though now the superficial is valued over the substantial, but his personal integrity can't be violated. Locs are not just for fashion; the hairstyle is a part of his heritage as well as a statement of pride, and it shows that being progressive is about investing in people and their identities, instead of only investing in how people make money. Concluding his big speech, Barker asserts that "whether or not I get the promotion I will not change my hair" (Browser & Wyatt 1994). Interestingly, his bosses didn't feel his locs were a problem; it was just Lawrence who brought it up to them and stated it was "unprofessional." In the end, Barker's bosses went ahead with the project and promoted him to funds manager.

Although Barker is a fictional character who experiences a fictional instance of discrimination against natural hair in the workforce, his story certainly still connects to the inequality that Black men and women with natural hair face in real life. Black sitcoms like *Living Single* show how representation mattered even in American media, which resonates with the social realities experienced by Black viewers.

In real life, though, there have been many reports of discrimination against natural hair taking place in schools and at school events as well. In 2018, a Buena Regional High School wrestler Andrew Johnson was told by referee Alan Maloney that he needed to cut off his locs or forfeit a match. Even though Johnson could have worn a head cover, the referee didn't allow it. In order not to forfeit the match, he agreed to cut his locs. The team trainer cut Johnson's hair, while his teammates, classmates, and school staff watched, and then Johnson won the match in overtime. The cutting of Johnson's locs was captured on video and was viewed millions of times after being posted online. After this incident, the referee was suspended by the New Jersey State Interscholastic Athletic Association. At that time, the association's executive director, Larry White, said the incident had hit close to home: "As an African American and parent — as well as a former educator, coach, official and athlete — I clearly understand the issues at play, and probably better than most. The NJSIAA takes this matter very seriously, and I ask that everyone respect the investigatory process related to all parties involved" (reported by Wamsley 2018). It has since been revealed that Maloney had been investigated on charges of racist conduct prior to this incident. In 2016, he apparently called another referee the N-word. Maloney has claimed that he doesn't remember using the slur; however, there are witnesses who said that he did. The New Jersey Wrestling Officials Association initially ordered that Maloney be suspended for a year, but he filed an appeal and the Association's ethics committee overturned the original suspension, ruling that it didn't have jurisdiction (reported by Wamsley 2018).

UNRAVELING THE STORY OF BLACK/AFRICAN HAIR

Dominic Speziali, the attorney for Johnson and his family, released a statement on behalf of his clients in which he brought up several items that add even further weight to Maloney's original ruling against Johnson's hair. Speziali reports that Maloney was in fact late to the meet and missed weigh-ins, when "scholastic wrestling rules clearly state that referees are to inspect wrestlers' appearance and determine any rules violations prior to the start of the meet, typically during weigh-ins" (reported by Wamsley 2018). Then, later, "[when] he did evaluate Johnson, he failed to raise any issues with the length of his hair or the need to wear a head covering" (reported by Wamsley 2018). Instead, Maloney prohibited the covering that Johnson wore over his locs, and then started the clock, giving the wrestler 90 seconds to cut his locs or forfeit the match. The family says, "Under duress but without any influence from the coaching staff or the athletic trainer, Andrew decided to have his hair cut rather than forfeit the match"(reported by Wamsley 2018. The family added that they are supportive of Buena's coaches and trainer: "The blame here rests primarily with the referee and those that permitted him to continue in that role despite clear evidence of what should be a disqualifying race-related transgression" (reported by Wamsley 2018).

Buena's school superintendent released a statement mentioning the incident and vowed continued support for its student-athletes. New Jersey's Department of Education stated that they have met with the NJSIAA and discussed "protecting the rights of all student-athletes across New Jersey" (reported by Wamsley 2018). The event also brought Johnson online support from Olympic gold-medal-winning wrestler Jordan Burroughs and film director Ava DuVernay, among others. Johnson's parents disclosed that the family had been moved by the outpouring of support, and that wrestling has taught their son resilience against adversity, saying that "As we move forward, we are comforted by both the strength of Andrew's character and the support he's received from the community. We will do all that we can to make sure that no student-athlete is forced to endure what Andrew experienced" (reported by Wamsley 2018).

High school student DeAndre Arnold from Texas

experienced another case of discrimination against natural hair. Like Johnson, he has locs, and Arnold reports that he has been wearing his since 7th grade. Barbers Hill Independent School District, which Arnold's high school is a part of, has a dress code. It verbalizes the usual things, such as the length of skirts and shorts, but it took further steps in regard to hair. Although the district allows locs, male students' hair cannot extend below the eyebrows or ear lobes; moreover, it rules that hairstyles must be kept shorter than the top of a T-shirt collar (Asmelash 2020). In order for Arnold to abide by the school dress code, he puts his hair up for school. For the duration of his four years at Barbers Hill, his locs hadn't been a problem. Suddenly, though, just before the winter break in December 2019, the district had some news for the Arnold family: cut the locks or face the consequences.

The school stated that Arnold couldn't walk at graduation if he continued to not follow the code. He would still be allowed to graduate, but he would be barred from spending the moment with his family and friends (reported by Asmelash 2020). While at school Arnold had been hit with in-school suspension (ISS). Sandy Arnold his mother stated, if her son wants to continue at the school, in-school suspension is his only option. Cutting his hair, though, is not an option. His father is from Trinidad, and growing locs is a common part of the culture. She said that: "He should get to choose who he identifies himself as, and he shouldn't be discriminated against. You don't tell girls they can't have short hair. It's so much bigger than DeAndre" (reported by Asmelash 2020). The school district does allow students to fill out exemption forms for medical or religious reasons, allowing students to break the dress code in special circumstances, and Ms. Arnold submitted the form after hearing about her son's dilemma with his locs. When asked why she had taken this long to take such action, her response was that she hadn't been aware an exemption form was even available.

As the situation gained more publicity, people across the country have called the policy racist. The story even reached the likes of actress Gabrielle Union, who tweeted her support for the teenager and told him to "keep fighting" against the "policing" of Black hair. On the other hand, Superintendent

Greg Poole told CNN the entire situation was false. "People want to call us racist, but we're following the rules, the law of the land," he said, arguing that the policy is fully within the realms of the law: "We're certainly not making this up" (reported by Asmelash 2020). Ms. Arnold, though, has said that she tried to work with the district. She has attempted to meet with Poole, and she also has shown up to board meetings and emailed members of the district's board of trustees. Ms. Arnold said she has been unable to make it onto the meeting agenda. Instead she's been relegated to speaking during the open forum, where she said she's given only a few minutes to make her case, she said (reported by Asmelash 2020). Poole went on to uphold the policy, calling it an "expectation of the community": high expectations lead to success, he said, and the dress code -- including the hair length rule -- is a part of that (reported by Asmelash 2020). When the school district tweeted that response, Dr. Bernice King countered the tweet, writing that "Arnold's locks do not reflect 'lowness' or a deviation from what should be a 'high expectation.'" Furthermore, Ibram X. Kendi, a professor and author of *How to Be an*

Antiracist, also retorted, writing that demanding a student to cut his dreadlocks actually holds students to a low standard of expectations. "There's nothing lower than teaching students to not respect cultural difference," (reported by Asmelash 2020). The school has told Ms. Arnold that the hair length policy is to help prevent distractions, she stated, "but she wonders who exactly his hair is distracting." "It's not keeping DeAndre from learning," she declared. "The only time I have to be in the office is concerning his hair. That's the distraction" (reported by Asmelash 2020).

According to the school's demographic report by *The Texas Tribune*, there are 169 Black students in the Barbers Hill Independent School District -- which consists of one high school, two middle schools, two elementary schools, one early childhood center, and one alternative educational program. Those students make up just 3.1% of the district's student population (Murphy and Daniel, 2019). When asked about the hair policy, Ms. Arnold questioned, "How much consideration do you think was made for that 3.1%? And I get it, that they don't understand Black natural hair. My point to get on the (meeting) agenda was to try to educate" (reported by Asmelash 2020). It has also been reported that none of the current members of the district's Board of Trustees are Black, though there has been a Black trustee in the past. When Poole was asked whether Black people were consulted about the policy, apart from the former board member, Poole simply echoed that the dress code is an expectation of the community. Furthermore Poole, who has been superintendent since 2006, claimed that this is the first time in his tenure the policy has impacted a Black student (reported by Asmelash 2020).

Less than a month after Arnold was banned from his prom and graduation unless he cut his locs, news of his story spread across on social media, with many celebrities and activists coming to Arnold's defense and encouraging him to stand up to his school's blatant discrimination against natural hair. Despite the ultimatum from his school, Arnold was honored with being an attendee at the 2020 Oscar awards, where he proudly wore his locs front and center. Arnold and his mother were invited to attend as the guests of director Matthew A. Cherry and producer Karen Toliver, who won the award for

Best Animated Short Film for *Hair Love*. Appropriately, *Hair Love* tells the story of an African American father learning to style his daughter's natural hair. Gabrielle Union, Dwyane Wade, and beauty brand Dove sponsored his tickets to the event, along with full wardrobe, hair, and makeup for him and his family (Diaz 2020). Furthermore, Arnold has received additional support of celebrities, like Ellen DeGeneres, who invited him to appear on her daytime show and surprised him with a $20,000 scholarship from Alicia Keys. Arnold has stated the scholarship will help him pursue his dream of becoming a veterinarian. He also said that "When Ellen said that school is supposed to be where you learn about cultures — not learn how to shut out cultures — that really stuck with me. . . The most exciting thing is seeing all the people that are on my side. I thought it would be a lot more hate than support" (reported by Diaz 2020). Lastly, Arnold maintained that "As teenagers, we have a voice and we're the future," he says. "I want more cultural acceptance. If there's any other situation that I feel like I need to stand up for, I would do that in a heartbeat" (reported by Diaz 2020).

UNRAVELING THE STORY OF BLACK/AFRICAN HAIR

In 2019, the CROWN Act was created to ensure protection against discrimination based on race-based hairstyles by extending statutory protection to hair texture and protective styles such as braids, locs, twists, and knots in the workplace and public schools. The CROWN Act stands for "Create a Respectful and Open World for Natural Hair." The bill was first introduced in California in January 2019 and signed into law on July 3, 2019. The CROWN Act expanded the definition of race in the Fair Employment and Housing Act (FEHA) and state Education Code, to ensure protection in workplaces and in K-12 public and charter schools. Since then, The CROWN Act has drawn support from federal and state legislators in the movement to end hair discrimination nationwide.

The second state to sign the Crown Act was New York. On July 12, 2019, Governor Andrew Cuomo signed into law S.6209A/A.7797A, which amends the Human Rights Law and Dignity for All Students Act to make clear that discrimination based on race includes hairstyles or traits associated with race. Governor Cuomo states, "For much of our nation's history, people of color - particularly women - have been marginalized and discriminated against simply because of their hair style or texture. By signing this bill into law, we are taking an important step toward correcting that history and ensuring people of color are protected from all forms of discrimination" (New York State 2019).

Then on December 19, 2019, Governor Phil Murphy of New Jersey also signed the CROWN Act. S3945, also known as the "Create a Respectful and Open Workplace for Natural Hair Act" (CROWN Act), which clarifies that prohibited race discrimination includes discrimination on the basis of "traits historically associated with race, including, but not limited to, hair texture, hair type, and protective hairstyles"(New Jersey State 2019). The law was introduced after Andrew Johnson, an African American high school wrestler at Buena Regional High School, was forced to cut off his dreadlocks in order to compete in a match on December 19, 2018 -- exactly one year before the bill was signed. "Race-based discrimination will not be tolerated in the State of New Jersey" said Governor Murphy. "No one should be made to feel uncomfortable or be discriminated against because of their natural hair. I am proud to sign this law in order to help ensure that all New Jersey residents can go to work, school, or participate in athletic events with dignity, he assured" (New Jersey State 2019). New Jersey is the third state to pass the CROWN Act, and recently, states such as Virginia, Maryland, Colorado, and Washington, plus cities such as Cincinnati, Ohio and Montgomery County, Maryland, have also joined them in passing the CROWN Act.

Today, eleven additional states are considering the CROWN Act and have either pre-filed, filed, or formally stated intent to introduce their own anti-hair discrimination bills. These states include Alabama, Arizona, Connecticut, Delaware, Georgia, Massachusetts, Michigan, Nebraska, Pennsylvania, Rhode Island, and Tennessee.

Chapter 7

Saye's Hair Story Part II

When I was a baby, my hair had a looser curl pattern, and as I grew, it became tighter. Along with my hair came shrinkage. As a child my hair was put in corn rows, twists, and hair bubbles, and it was washed every two to three weeks. I couldn't stand that part because of the process. My hair regimen included shampooing and conditioning, then deep conditioning or doing a protein treatment. After that part, pink moisturizer and Blue Magic hair grease was applied to my hair. I do remember how dreadful detangling was because the comb used wasn't wide enough for my thick tresses.

Despite all of this, I never really took notice of my hair until I was in grade school. During that time, we were living in the Poconos, PA after moving from Far Rockaway, Queens, NY. Back then there weren't many Black people or POC on that mountain, and in school you would be the only Black person in the classroom or 1 of 4 Black students. My white classmates would be fascinated with my hair and want to touch it. Some would make comments such as, "why is your hair like that?" or "your hair feels like a brillo pad or wool." So even at that young age I began to wonder why my hair was the way it was. One day I asked my mother why my hair stuck up: by my memory, it must have been a style like an afro at the time. From my remembrance of the question, she answered by saying that it was the type of hair that sub-Saharan Africans and people of sub-Saharan African descent have: because we are originally from a hot climate, our hair grows up in order to help us stay cool.

As far as I was concerned, though, I just wanted my hair to be different. Plus, my mother and sister's hair were relaxed. My sister in particular had started getting a relaxer at the age of five. When I asked my mother about relaxing my hair, she said she didn't want that for my hair, but at the time I didn't like her explanation. I just felt left out because their hair was "silky straight" and mine was "kinky wooly." While in school I started seeing some of my Black friends having their hair relaxed and that drove me insane because I couldn't get one. Although my hair was being taken good care of by the women in my life, I yearned for a relaxer.

There was a girl who was in the 6th grade and she had a sister who was in the second grade with me. She always would brag to my sister, my sister's friend, and myself about how her sister had "good hair" who didn't need a perm because it was straight and long. As we were walking one day, she told my sister's friend that I had nappy hair and needed a perm because I looked busted. She didn't realize that I overheard what she said, but I had and the comment about my hair being "nappy" scarred me for a long time, just making me more determined about wanting my hair relaxed. I continued to bother my mother about relaxing my hair and of course she said no, explaining that she wanted my hair to grow out more. Surprisingly, she did allow me to get my hair braided with extensions.

I was eight years old when I first got box braids. I was so happy because I was able to have longer hair and swing the braids. For the 1998-1999 school year my hair was mostly in braids. When I removed the extensions and washed my hair, I couldn't stand the shrinkage I saw because my hair looked like a TWA. After my hair was washed, my sister flat ironed my hair and I was happy to see it straight and with length, even temporarily; on the other hand, though, it wasn't a perm. When summer 1999 rolled around, I asked my mother if she would perm my hair, and this time she said she would think about it. That was music to my ears because the years prior to, she didn't want my hair chemically straightened at all. One day we went to Rite-Aid and bought Beautiful Beginnings children's relaxer. For a whole week the relaxer just sat on my desk because my mother dreaded relaxing my hair. After me pleading with her once more, my mother finally decided to give me my first relaxer. What I find funny, looking back, is that when my sister's friend came to visit I even got her to see the main event of my hair being relaxed. Finally, at the age of nine my hair was relaxed and I crossed the rights of passage. I couldn't stop playing with my hair from where it sat near my collar bone. It was extremely easy to say good-bye to my natural hair. While my hair was relaxed, it could be done up in buns, ponytails, and even braids right before touch-ups.

As I enjoyed this new style, though, my hair started to break and the back of my hair quickly became shorter than the front. When I put my hair up, I would have to pin the back; so that it wouldn't get out of place. Despite my hair being relaxed, I started to feel self-conscious about my hair due to the breakage and unevenness. There was an instance where two of my classmates in 4th grade constantly criticized me about my hair. They kept talking about my hair being short, to the point that I became annoyed and yelled "so what?" Then one of them said it is okay to have short hair. I said, then why are you all keep saying how short my hair is? Ironically, they didn't have the longest hair either. Looking back to this view of hair, I can see now that living in an area where there wasn't much representation of girls who looked like us, all while seeing white girls or non-Black POC girls constantly being complimented on their long flowing hair, would definitely make anyone feel insecure about their hair – let alone a little girl my age at the time!

In the fall of the year that I was going to 5th grade, my mother finally took me to the hair salon for the first time. I was ecstatic for that experience because I had seen my mother and sister going from time to time. The service I was going to receive there was, of course, a perm. The kind of hairstyle I asked for was Shirley Temple curls with bangs. During this first salon visit, the hairstylist stated she was going to trim my hair; however, she became scissor happy and cut off 2-3 inches of my hair. What made matters worse, I didn't get the Shirley Temple curls, but the "bumper curl" hairstyle instead. When my mom picked me up that day, I cried because I wasn't happy with my hair. My mother assured me that my hair would grow back and we could style my hair another way. When I got home, I rolled my bangs and put my hair half up, half down. Then the hair that was down, my mother rolled it so that I could have the Shirley Temple curls.

When I started 5th grade, I felt somewhat better about my hair and my classmates complimented me on my new look. Even better, in my class there were Black girls with perms, crochet hair, and, what struck me the most, was one with locs. I admired her hair even though I didn't care for my own. Back in 2000-2001 I didn't see many Black girls with natural hair, since most had it pressed straight. But I always loved how that one classmate's locs would curl when they were rolled with flexi or perm rods. She showed me that natural hair can be pretty as well.

The summer before I was headed to junior high, my hair was in cornrow extensions. That was a protective style for me because while spending the summer with my late maternal grandparents I would go swimming in their pool a lot. When I removed the braiding extensions at the end of that summer, my hair was actually transitioning and I could have returned natural then. At the time, though, I still preferred a relaxer. I remember my late maternal grandmother complimenting my hair and greasing it with Vaseline because she ran out of hair grease. She put my hair in two French braids. Honestly, though, I couldn't wait for my late maternal aunt to perm my hair so I could have the bone-straight hair I had admired and wanted for so long. I was so happy to get a relaxer from my aunt and my hair had grown back from that time when I was unlucky enough to get a scissor-happy hair stylist. This time I received a trim and my Aunt gave me a blunt cut, which I loved. We also discussed how my hair could remain healthy. Some of the tips were deep conditioning, protein treatments, moisturizing, and wrapping my hair up, as well as keeping my ends healthy through treatments such as trimming them every 6-8 weeks or if I had split ends. At that time I was eleven, so it would have been her, my mother, sister, or other women relatives who were trimming my hair. That summer I experimented with styles such as flat twists, buns, roller sets, and Bantu knots. When I started 6th grade, I felt comfortable with my hair and I did cute hairstyles. The only thing that bothered me was the back of my hair being shorter than the rest of my hair.

One day I wore my hair half up and half down and a classmate whispered to someone that my hair was short and ugly. Again, that made me feel down and have a negative view of my hair. Another classmate called my hair "nappy" on a day when I had my hair up in a bun because my hair kitchen (hair at the nape of my neck) was kinky and needed a touch-up. This time around, though, I didn't just sit there and take the remarks: instead, I responded and I told this classmate that he needed to have his hair re-braided because it looked old. That remark kept him quiet. When I came back to school later, my hair was relaxed and styled with half in a bun and the other half curled. As I walked to class that day, a classmate told me I had "pretty hair." I was astonished because I would rarely get that kind of compliment with my hair, particularly because back then with the kinky hair texture that I have, this wouldn't have been considered "good hair." At the time, if your hair was shoulder-waist length or of a looser curl, then that was deemed "pretty hair." So I smiled and said thank you to my classmate. Whatever beauty she saw within my hair, I wasn't able to discover it.

 When I began leaving childhood and coming into adolescence, I looked to my sister because she was leaving that stage and coming into her womanhood. She understood the good and bad of your teenage years. I was impressed by how she groomed and cared for her hair. Many times during that period, I would have her style my hair in "cute styles." When she did my hair, it always boosted my confidence level. During that time, she would put her hair in micro-braids when she wanted a break from the relaxer. I also saw how the braids grew her actual hair, due to it being a form of protective styling. On the other hand, from my sister I learned that with this style you have to be extra careful that it isn't too tight around your edges and be extra careful during take-down. Then make sure you are clarifying your hair and doing a protein treatment. Since my sister was mindful of these things, she was able to achieve length retention.

    For 7th grade, my sister styled my hair in micro-braids and I was able to give my real hair a break. That school year my signature mark was my micro-braids and some of my classmates referred to me as Brandy. I took that as an endearment because she is one of my favorite singers and she effortlessly "rocked" her cornrows, box braids, and micro-

Saye's Hairstory Part II

braids throughout the mid-1990s and early 2000s. From time to time she would take us back to her *Moesha* days and wear her famous box braids. That same year, though, I also began to observe how critical peers were toward each other in middle school and I would hear comments about how I was probably "bald" or my hair was extremely "short" because I always wore braids. Of course, that isn't always the case, since you can have shoulder-waist length hair and wear wigs or extensions. A particular classmate even asked if I used Rogaine, a popular baldness treatment for my hair. The funny thing about this is that I learned later, he was told to say that by another classmate who was evidently too much of a coward to say that to my face.

UNRAVELING THE STORY OF BLACK/AFRICAN HAIR

The classmates making those remarks, especially the Black classmates, were those who failed to realize the uniqueness of Black/African hair. Now with the natural hair movement and awareness of Black hair, some have become enlightened. There was a scenario where I was being criticized because my braids were getting fuzzy due to new growth. One of my friends stated that it looks like I have been in a fight and another joined and said the braids needed to remove. The "quiet" Saye broke out of her shell and yelled "you both are due for a perm while you want to make comments about my braids."

Another part of my hair I got teased by was my sideburns. This stemmed from rapper Lloyd Banks who had made a reference about Rhythm and Blues singer Ashanti's sideburns. This was also during the time when there were discrepancies between rappers Ja-Rule and 50 Cent. One day at school a classmate started saying that I had "Ashanti side burns" after they heard Lloyd Bank's song. That was the big joke on me for that class period. I didn't pay attention because I loved my sideburns then, and I still do to this day. Back then

Saye's Hairstory Part II

I used Softsheen-Carson Let's Jam! Shining and Conditioning Gel or Ampro Style Protein Styling Gel to slick my side burns. Now I have been using Creme of Nature Argan Oil Perfect Edges. I come from a family where we are hairy, so it was completely expected to have thick or long sideburns. A couple years ago Ashanti did address the jokes regarding her sideburns on the New York City radio show *The Breakfast Club*. She stated, "Some people love sideburns. So this is what I thought. On TV, on film and in pictures, it looks a little different but when you [are] looking in the mirror ... you know, you're gelling it down, you know it's soft," she told Angela Yee, DJ Envy, and Charlemagne Tha God. She said that "But on film and on camera, it may look a little different... it looks a little funny... So [now] I just make sure they look good on film, and on camera, and in person" (Ashanti 2014).

Before 7th grade ended, though, I changed my hairstyle again and went back to wearing it in a relaxer. When I came to school the first time after doing this, some of my classmates were in awe because they'd gotten the idea that I didn't have hair. Those who knew me before knew how my hair looked like. The same person who made a reference about the Rogaine now asked if I had a weave and my friends came to my defense, saying it was my own hair. I even split my hair in the middle to show that it was actually my hair. It wasn't in its natural state then, but it was my real hair. I was told by both my male and female classmates that I looked better with my real hair rather than extensions. I said that "I like both styles and I didn't care want you all think." When the weather began to change it started being humid and my relaxed hair was "poofy." I observed my sister using the CareFree Curl Snap Back Curl Restorer and saw how it gave her hair a curly effect. During that time, our mother was using the Wave Nouveau curly perm. She would also use the Snap Back Curl Restorer for her hair when she started receiving new growth. After I saw the results from my sister, I decided to give it a try. I loved how the product gave me a curl definition. At the time, that was the farthest I was going to get when it came to returning natural.

    In the beginning of 8th grade, I wore my hair in cornrow styles, giving my hair a break through this protective styling. Although braids have been a part of our history, I observed

Saye's Hairstory Part II

that some of Black classmates would make subtle remarks about others' hair if it wasn't relaxed or out flowing. For me, I always appreciated versatility with hairstyles because this is a part of our culture. After I wore my hair in corn rows, I relaxed my hair and had that style for a while. I would put sheen spray in my hair, which led to some of my white classmates asking why my hair was so shiny. I mentioned that I used a hairspray for Black people, which has oil in it because our hair needs that, and one of my non-Black classmates attempted to touch my hair. I moved my head away because, as many Black women and girls know, this has been an issue for a long time. Non-Black people are often amazed at our hair and they touch it without our consent, violating personal boundaries. Though I understand that some people don't mean any harm, that still doesn't make it all right to do, particularly without asking, and even then, the harm can be subtle based on history. Moreover, there should always be a conversation about asking for permission to touch one's hair. At the time, I deal with this by politely telling my classmate to not touch my hair without asking. She then asked and I did allow her to touch my hair.

UNRAVELING THE STORY OF BLACK/AFRICAN HAIR

Before Christmas break that year, I did a wash and set with my hair. I washed and deep conditioned it, then put in moisturizer and added setting oil so that I could put it in rollers. I then went under the *Golden Hot* hooded dryer, and after all that, I came out with a nice drop-curled hairstyle. When I went to school wearing it, I received compliments like "Saye, you should wear your hair like this more often," and I said, I will. Though of course, there were also people who came with their "joking" remarks, such as "Saye, you look like Oprah with your hairstyle." I didn't care what they thought about my hair, though, and that's how I got them off me. Evidently, these kinds of remarks are based on those people not feeling good about themselves.

During the spring that year, I decided to sign up for afterschool swimming classes held at Pocono Mountain West High School (PMWHS) along with my friends. The swim class was fun, but it did take a toll on my hair. One time on my way home on the afterschool activity bus, I had covered my head with my coat hood because I was embarrassed at the "poofiness" of my hair. Two upperclassmen asked why I had my hood on, so I said that my hair was "nappy" after swim class. Two of my swim mates said that their hair was "nappy" as well, and one of them added, "You have an excuse; you are Black." Everyone busted out laughing. My swimmate who made that comment was Latina, most likely of Taino and African descent. To be honest, the way she said it was hilarious to me. In this case the usage of the word "nappy" was not based on kinky coily hair texture, and more on the way all of our hair appeared from the chlorine. Honestly, this shared experience made all the difference, showing how the same word can be used by different people in different situations so that one is all right, and even funny, while others are hurtful and mean.

    That swim class was two days a week, and after each class I had to wash, condition and protein treat my hair because of the chlorine, plus my hair was relaxed. Unfortunately, I became careless and slacked on this care routine, and by the time I graduated 8th grade, I had developed a slight bald spot at the mid-scalp region of my head. Thankfully, I was able to cover that spot up with hair near it. During that time my mother was working in Philadelphia, so when she came home and saw what happened, she was hysterical. I explained that it was from swimming and not taking proper care of my hair. We both took a trip to the beauty supply store and bought a product called 911 Emergency Hair Treatment Leave In Conditioner. Once a day I would apply it to my bald spot. Two weeks after I used it, I started to see growth from that area of my hair, and by the start of high school, that spot of my hair was catching up with the rest. However, I had learned my lesson to not be complacent with my hair. Next time if I was going swimming, I would put my hair in a protective style or wear two swimming caps over it.

  After that incident with my hair, I began to pay more attention to it, even though I continued to have it relaxed. I observed that my hair would grow to my shoulders and then it would break off. I also received a lot of shedding and scalp burns from the relaxer, and I would have scabs throughout my hair. I despised going through these ups and downs with my hair. There was even a point when I felt like shaving off all my hair and just starting out fresh, but I didn't want to be ridiculed by my schoolmates, and this would have been the time it happened, since bullying often occurs during adolescence if you appear "different."

After the end of 9th grade my parents decided to move away from the Poconos. Although I missed my friends dearly, I was glad for us to move. In regards to my family, the Poconos was a good starting point after we left Far Rockaway; however, as time passed, it was best that we relocate to metropolitan New Jersey. During the last two years of high school, I continued to battle with my hair. Around 2006, I discovered the kinky twist hairstyle, which I saw some of my classmates wearing and found to be very cute. The style includes a two-strand twist with extensions that fall around chin to shoulder length. It also requires curling the ends with perm rods or rollers and soaking them in hot water, then removing the rods after the ends have cooled. You also have the option to use your own hair; however, skip soaking your real hair in hot water.

I always loved this hairstyle because it looked good on me and it wasn't as time-consuming as the micro-braids. While living in Elizabeth, New Jersey I saw a lot of my classmates

UNRAVELING THE STORY OF BLACK/AFRICAN HAIR

wearing their natural hair. Some would flat iron or hot comb their hair as well. I was amazed to see so many of my school mates proudly rocking their type 4 hair. Before that, I had only seen those with the looser curl pattern or "good hair" wearing their hair in its natural state. Anyone with kinky hair would have it straightened, and everyone had relaxers. Now I saw all of this, and more; I also saw girls who wore braids. However your hair was, it was celebrated. Furthermore, I enjoyed the infusion of cultures within our new Elizabeth community as well. I can only think of one issue I had regarding my hair at the time. After I took out my kinky twist and went back to having a relaxer, my hair stylist at the time gave me a bob cut. When I came back to school, my schoolmates admired my new cut, except for one who made subtle remarks, before I said that her hair looked like a mop. Then she said that she would take all the shine away from me. I stated that I wasn't in a competition with her. The reason why she attacked me is because when she came with a haircut some classmates didn't take notice and when they observed my hair, she felt left out. Again, when you are in high school, there is drama and people want to compete with you. It becomes dangerous when you put somebody down in order to make yourself feel good or to seek attention.

After the cut my hair was shoulder length and I didn't suffer from breakage again until I was about 18, when it began breaking off again because of the chemicals from the relaxers. I was told that my hair was breaking, but by that point I already knew that. My issue was that, if you are so concerned about my hair, why not share with me the products that help with healthier hair? In addition, your diet plays a part of your hair health, and I just didn't know this at the time. Right before my senior prom, I put kinky twists in my hair to give my real hair a break, and because of this choice, I was able to start growing out my hair.

When I started college, I tried a texturizer with my hair, which I found didn't give me scalp burns or much breakage. However, I did observe that my hair was thin. Then, towards the end of 2008, I got my first sew-in weave, which was a blunt cut since I didn't care for a long weave down my back. A piece of my hair was left out so that it could look natural. Since

I was transitioning back to natural hair, I flat ironed that section so that I could blend in with the weave. If I had known better, I would have asked for a full closure to avoid that part receiving heat damage. When my hair was in a texturizer, it curled slightly but still appeared mostly straight. Interestingly, I'd finally gotten the curl look that I wanted while being natural. Apparently, if I used gel or curl enhancing products for natural hair, it brought out the curl pattern for my hair type. While texturized, though, my hair didn't have body and it appeared limp.

During Summer 2009, I was very frustrated with my hair and I put kinky twists in for a couple of months, giving it a break from the manipulation and chemicals. The last relaxer I had was April 2010 and from then on, I started transitioning and looking into returning natural. I was eager to work on a new journey with my hair after watching a YouTube video that showcased type 4 hair. From May 2010-March 2011 I wore braids and weaves. In between, I would put my real hair in double strand twists or buns. It was difficult to work with the two different hair textures in my hair, but after a while of doing this, I finally caught a peek of my hair and realized how close I was getting to going back natural.

Before stepping into this journey, I decided to get a Dominican blow out, which involves a wash and deep conditioning and then a roller set. Once the roller set is removed, a heat protectant is applied, which is key. A blowdryer and round brush is used to straighten your hair. The last step is a "Doobie" or wrap, which involves your hair being wrapped around your head and then bobby pins being used to keep the wrap in place. The "Doobie" helps to keep your hair straight and gives it movement.

When my hair was being styled this way, though, the hair stylist referred to it as "Pelo Malo" (bad hair) and that infuriated me. She didn't realize that I understood some Spanish and I am aware of the trauma of that phrase. "Pelo Malo" is just as damaging as "nappy hair." I explained to the stylist I knew what that word meant and she used it because I have a tighter curl pattern. She was somewhat embarrassed and asked if I spoke Spanish. I said *un poquito* (a little). What we fail to realize is that only damaged, unhealthy hair is "bad" –

otherwise, hair of any type that is healthy and growing is good hair. Hair texture does not define whether hair is bad or good. When the stylist finished my hair, everyone said *muy bonita* (very pretty). Yes, I thought to myself, the hairstyle was nice, but was it perceived as pretty because it was straight?

While at work after receiving this style, my co-workers were impressed by how much hair I had. They asked why I was wearing weaves or braiding extensions before, and I explained that I was transitioning and growing out my hair. One of my workmates thought my hair was a wig cap and I said touch it, then: when they did, they discovered that it clearly wasn't a wig. It can be annoying when Black women and girls who naturally have long hair have to prove or show that it is our own. Black women and girls have long hair as well. With the type of hair we have it shrinks, so it can often appear shorter than it really is. Due to the chemicals of the relaxers and excess manipulation, some of us experience hair breakage and that is another factor to the notion of us not having "long hair." My husband, who was my boyfriend then, always liked my hair, but at the time he preferred the kinky twist and curly weave that I had had prior. My hair was healthy and it was thriving.

In order for my hair to remain this way, the next step was returning truly natural. The back of my hair had already returned natural and the front was showing some relaxed ends. So, two weeks later, I went back to the hair salon for the stylist to cut my hair, and on March 2011, I had finally returned natural. At first I didn't wear my hair in its natural state. I had it straightened and it was down to my jawline before it was shoulder length. Once it was time to wash my hair, it reverted back natural and I was not turning back. The start of my journey had its share of trial and error because the last time my hair had been natural, I was 9 years old, and this time I was 21. I had to get to know my hair again. Despite the challenges, internally I was extremely confident with my natural hair and I was ready to embrace her. When my mother saw my hair, she loved it immediately: my hair now took her back to how it had looked when I was just a child. I received a lot of compliments with my hair despite the fact I was still learning how to style and care for it.

In the beginning my husband, who was my boyfriend,

didn't like the new look. Keep in mind, many Black women hair were permed, in braids, or weaves. On the other hand, he liked when I did twist outs. After I went natural, my mother and sister started their journeys as well. I believe if their hair was natural when I was a little girl, I may have not thought about wanting my hair relaxed. However, I still could have asked for one based on seeing school mates with relaxed hair.

At the start of my natural hair journey, I looked to the YouTube natural hair influencers. I was able to see what their hair regimens were and what natural hair products to use. The first few years of my journey, I spent a lot of money on products that was not necessary. Over time, though, I realized that less was more. Having type 4 hair, I learned that my hair needed lots of moisture and it became dry easily. I had to incorporate the LCO method in my hair care routine, and I found that water-based moisturizers, thick butters, and sealing my hair with JBCO worked best for my hair. Initially, I was against using hair grease because of the myths about it not being good for your hair. I used natural oils such as coconut oil, olive oil, or tea tree oil. The tea tree oil helped with the itchiness; however, I needed something for the dryness. It was recommended that I used sulfur 8 grease for my scalp. I was hesitant to use it at first, but then I remembered that my mother had used it for my scalp while I was growing up. I gave it a try and my scalp felt so much better. For the type of scalp I have, grease has been a better choice compared to the natural oils. So now I just use the natural oils on my hair to seal in the moisture. Throughout my hair journey, I discovered that the products or hair regimen that works for others may not work for me and vice versa.

In the spring of 2014, I had the pleasure of attending my first natural hair meet-up event. The theme was Naturals in the Park at The Highline in New York City, hosted by Locs Revolution and Bella Kinks. The event really captured the beauty of African and African diaspora people. Our hidden commonalities were revealed through the experience we have with our hair. Barbados, Dominican Republic, Ghana, Guyana, Grenada, Haiti, Liberia, St. Vincent and the Grenadines, Trinidad and Tobago, and the United States all came together to celebrate Black/African natural hair.

My experience didn't stop with this one event, though. While working at the Elizabeth Public Library (EPL) in New Jersey, a *Hair for All* exhibition was created. I helped set-up the mini museum that captured the history and beauty of Black/African hair. In 2015, I also had the opportunity to help with a natural hair event at EPL. In honor of Women's History Month, former colleagues and I presented the *Good Hair* film and discussion. Attendees viewed the hair documentary and had the chance to share stories about their own hair. Overall, it was a great turn out, and participants enjoyed both the film and the mini presentation on Black hair. They were all able to receive a hair product or styling tool. As a group, my workmates and I discussed how we care for our hair. This program was fitting because many Black women and girls were returning natural, and we got to talk about how it was more than just a trend: it was a part of our identity.

Around the same time, I was getting ready for my wedding and my mind was already made up that I was going to wear my hair natural. For my bridesmaids and the rest of my wedding party, I wanted them to style their hair however felt comfortable and beautiful to them—when it comes to women's hair, you want it to be done in a way that makes them look and feel good. As for me, I was not doing the traditional press and curl style that was usual for special occasions. Plus, my wedding was down south in June and it rained on the big day. Everyone asked how I was going to style my hair and my response was either that it would be a natural hairstyle or that it was a surprise. Although returning natural was on the rise then, there was still a subconscious perception that natural hair wouldn't look good for big occasions like this. Prior to my wedding, I viewed many natural hairstyles for special occasions and they all looked beautiful. I was in year four of my natural hair journey then, and all I could see was myself with a spectacular style in my natural hair. I sent some ideas to my aunt who is a professional hairstylist and was going to style my hair. When my wedding day came, I was actually calm and not too emotional. My hair was done beautifully in a twisted up do hairstyle with double strand twists on the side.

UNRAVELING THE STORY OF BLACK/AFRICAN HAIR

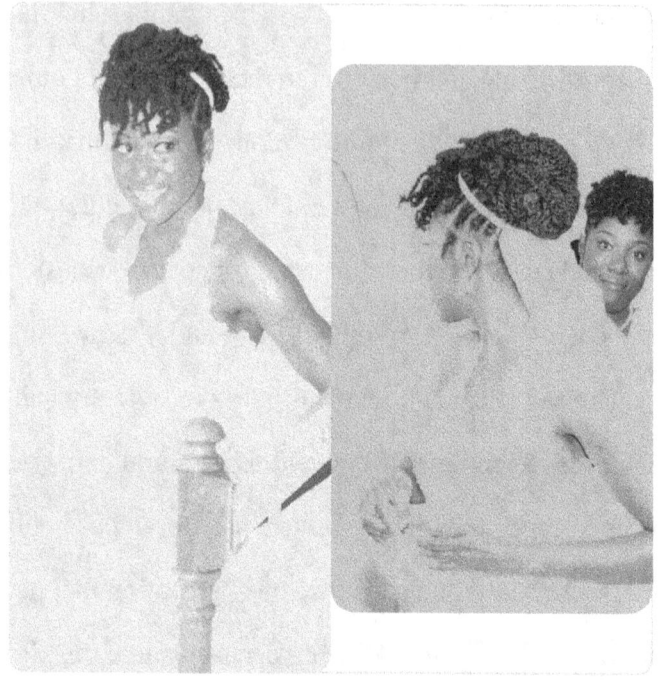

Hair styled by Cat, owner and hairstylist of
Pure 1 Hair Studio. Richmond, Texas

The styles worn by my flower girl, junior bridesmaids, and bridesmaids all reflected the diversity of Black hair and hairstyles that have been a part of our heritage.

Saye's Hairstory Part II

Within the past five years, I've been keeping my hair regimen simple as compared to when I first returned natural. Every two weeks (twice a month during the wintertime), I wash my hair with Renpure Coconut Cream Nourishing Shampoo followed by the Renpure conditioner. I then deep condition my hair with Aunt Jackie's Coconut Crème Deep Conditioner. Once a month I do a protein treatment either with Aphogee two-step protein treatment or with mayonnaise. For a leave-in conditioner I use Aunt Jackie's Knot on My Watch, and afterwards I grease my scalp with Sulfur 8 Light Formula hair grease. The moisturizer that I use for my hair at any given time depends on the style I am planning to wear it in next. If I plan on wearing a twist out, for instance, I will twist my hair with Cream of Nature Pure Honey Moisture Whip Twisting Cream or use Adwoa Beauty Baomint Moisturizing curl defining cream, then seal my hair with Tropic Isle Living JBCO. Within 48 hours I unravel my hair and wear a twist out. The twist out lasts for a whole week and at night I only twist two strands in the front of my hair, then put my hair in a bonnet. In the morning I brush my edges and nape areas and use a little bit of edge control. When I put my hair in buns, braided, or twisted

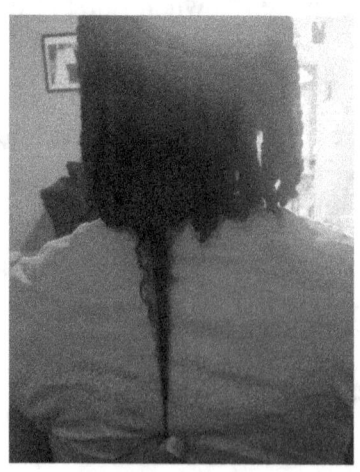

updos, I will moisturize my hair with Organic Root Stimulator (ORS) olive oil hair lotion and seal with JBCO.

Finally, two or three times a year I visit my hair stylist for trimming, flat ironing, or protective styles such as crochet, cornrow extensions, or braided updos with my natural hair.

In the year 2020, I am so proud of how far I have come with my hair. As a little girl and as a teenager, I didn't appreciate my hair. At the age of thirty, though, I embrace everything about my hair. What I like about my hair includes its shrinkage, kinkiness, poofiness, boldness, and versatility. While some of these things might be seen as negatives, I have come to see the positive in them all. As time passed, I began to appreciate my hair shrinkage and allow my hair to be. Also, shrinkage is a part of what makes curly, kinky, coily, and afro textured hair astonishing. Shrinkage is a sign of healthy hair because it shows that your hair is properly moisturized and has good elasticity.

This year also marks my ninth into my natural hair journey. Now that I am a mother to a bright and adorable son, I want him to know that kinky, coily, and afro textured hair is beautiful as well. If God blesses me and my husband with a daughter, then she will see me happily rocking my natural hair and viewing the magnificence of natural hair. When she reaches the point where she can make her own decisions, I will support whatever way she decides that she wants to wear her hair. On the other hand, I will stress the importance of keeping your hair and scalp healthy, which involves daily and monthly hair maintenance, plus your overall health such as diet and exercise.

In closing, I want the history of Black/African hair to be better known. I also want more people to become aware of how far we have come with our hair, which is so distinctive because it is a reflection of Mother Nature. The styles and techniques made possible by Black hair have been innovative.

However you wear your hair, let it be based on choice and how it makes you feel, not on anyone's views or negative historical depictions. Regardless of your hair texture, hair that is healthy will always be good hair. And as long as you take care of your hair, your tresses will flourish.

UNRAVELING THE STORY OF BLACK/AFRICAN HAIR

References

References Chapter 1

Adams, M. V. (2005). *The multicultural imagination: race, color, and the unconscious.* Routledge.

Ballinger, W. (2007). Why African Americans Try to Obtain Good Hair. Sociological Viewpoints. PDF. Retrieved March 16, 2014, from http://www.pasocsociety.org/bellinger.pdf

Brown, A. & A. Knapp. (2006). *NPS Ethnography: African American Heritage & Ethnography.* National Parks Service, U.S. Department of the Interior. Retrieved January 15, 2020, from https://www.nps.gov/ethnography/aah/aaheritage/FrenchAmA.htm.

Byrd, A. D. & L. L. Tharps. (2001). *Hair story: untangling the roots of Black hair in America.* St Martin's Press.

Chamberlain, G. (2012). *Madam C.J. Walker.* The Black Inventor Online Museum. Retrieved March 12, 2014, from http://blackinventor.com/madam-c-j-walker/

Dione-Rosado, S. (2008). No Nubian knots or nappy locks: discussing the politics of hair among women of African descent in the Diaspora. A Report on Research in Progress. *Transforming Anthropology, 11*(2), 60-63. https://doi.org/10.1525/tran.2003.11.2.60

Engel, E. (n.d.) *Annie Malone*. Historic Missourians, The State Historical Society of Missouri. Retrieved April 17, 2020, from https://historicmissourians.shsmo.org/historicmissourians/name/m/malone/#intro

Everett, D. E. (1966). Free Persons of color in colonial Louisiana. *Louisiana History: The Journal of the Louisiana Historical Association, 7* (1), 21-50. Retrieved January 15, 2020, from http://www.jstor.org/stable/4230881

Fihlani, P. (2016, June 11). *How South African women are reclaiming the headscarf.* BBC News, BBC. Retrieved August 21, 2018, from www.bbc.com/news/world-africa-36461213.

The History Makers (2003, December 18). *George Johnson | The HistoryMakers.* Retrieved April 15, 2014, from http://www.thehistorymakers.com/biography/george-johnson-38

hooks, b. (1995). *Killing Rage.* H. Holt & Company.

References

Little, K. L. (1948). The Poro society as an arbiter of culture. *African Studies* 7 (1), 1-15. https://doi.org/10.1080/00020184808706749

Matshego, L. (2020, January 24). *A history of African women's hairstyles*. Africa.com. Retrieved July 18, 2020 from www.africa.com/history-african-womens-hairstyles/.

Michals, D. (2015). *Madam C. J. Walker*. National Women's History Museum. National Women's History Museum, 2015. Retrieved March 29, 2020 from https://www.womenshistory.org/education-resources/biographies/madam-cj-walker

Nittle, N. (2019, February 15). *Annie Malone: She became a millionaire after giving Madam C.J. Walker her big break as a sales agent*. The Goods, Vox. Retrieved April 17, 2020, from https://www.vox.com/the-goods/2019/2/15/18226396/annie-turnbo-malone-hair-entrepreneur-trump-black-history

Patton, T. O. (2006). Hey girl, am I more than my hair?: African American women and their struggles with beauty, body image, and hair. *NWSA Journal, 18* (2), 24-51.

Schleier, C. (2018, June 4). *Annie Turnbo Established A Hair Care Empire For African-American Women.* LEADERS & SUCCESS, Investor's Business Daily, Retrieved April 17, 2020, from https://www.investors.com/news/management/leaders-and-success/annie-turnbo-built-hair-care-empire-for-african-american-women/

Sieber, R., & Herreman, F. (2000). Hair in African Art and Culture. African Arts, 33(3), 55-96. doi:10.2307/3337689

Thirteen – Media with Impact. (2004). *Slavery and the Making of America.* The Slave Experience: Men, Women & Gender.PBS. Retrieved August 21, 2018, from www.thirteen.org/wnet/slavery/experience/gender/feature6.html.

Thompson, C. (2009). Black women and identity: what's hair got to do with it? *Michigan Feminist Studies 22* (1): special issue Politics and Performativity. Mpublishing. Retrieved March 16, 2014, from http://quod.lib.umich.

References

edu/cgi/t/text/text-idx?cc=mfsfront;c=mfs;c=mfsfront;i dno=ark5583.0022.105;rgn=main;view=text;xc=1;g=mfsg.

American Academy of Dermatology. (n.d.). *What Kids Should Know about How Hair Grows*. American Academy of Dermatology Association. Retrieved May 16, 2020, from www.aad.org/public/parents-kids/healthy-habits/parents/kids/hair-grows.

References Chapter 2

Addo, J.R. (n.d.) *About the Founder*. Adwoa Beauty. Retrieved July 29, 2019, from https://www.adwoabeauty.com/pages/about-the-founder

Arlexis, S. (2017, June 4). 7 heat-free ways to stretch natural hair." Bustle. Retrieved January 6, 2020, from https://www.bustle.com/p/7-heat-free-ways-to-stretch-natural-hair-defeat-shrinkage-once-for-all-58827.

Miss BB. (2016, May 13). African Hair Threading – History and Tutorial. Black and Beautiful. Retrieved January 2, 2020, from https://blackandbeautiful.fr/blog/

en/2016/05/13/hair-threading-history-and-tutorial/.

Berg, M. (2019, February 21). *These mother-and-son entrepreneurs went from selling soap on Harlem streets to an $850 million fortune."* Forbes, Forbes Magazine. Retrieved July 29, 2019, from www.forbes.com/sites/maddieberg/2018/09/21/these-black-entrepreneurs-went-from-selling-soap-on-harlem-streets-to-a-850-million-fortune/#7b4b0eed4b14.

Brown, R. (2020, March 16). Adwoa Beauty set to launch prestige texture haircare at Sephora. Brand Report, Beauty Independent. Retried March 21, 2020, from https://www.beautyindependent.com/adwoa-beauty-launch-prestige-textured-haircare-at-sephora/

Contreras, C. (2017, April 11). Yo Amo Mi Pajón: Loving Natural Hair In The Dominican Republic. Interviewed by Mariana Dale for 91.5 KJZZ. Retrieved February 7, 2020, from https://kjzz.org/content/458504/yo-amo-mi-paj%C3%B3n-loving-natural-hair-dominican-republic

Contreras, C. (n.d.). *"Our Story.* Miss Rizos. Retrieved February 7, 2020, from https://www.missrizos.com/en/

References

nosotros/

Diaz, T. (2019, April 4). *Miss Rizos is finally bringing her curly salon to the U.S.* Beauty, Refinery 29. Retrieved February 7, 2020 from, https://www.refinery29.com/en-us/2019/04/228827/miss-rizos-salon-new-york-city

Easter, M. (2017, August 10). *Money flowing into the natural hair industry is a blessing and curse for those who built it up."* Los Angeles Times. Retrieved July 29, 2019, from www.latimes.com/business/la-fi-natural-hair-industry-20170809-htmlstory.html#.

Hill, S. (2019, January 11). *Shea Moisture founder Richelieu Dennis to tTurn Madam C.J. Walker's estate into a center for Black women entrepreneurs.* Black Enterprise. Retrieved January 7, 2020, from https://www.blackenterprise.com/shea-moisture-richelieu-dennis-madam-cj-walker/

Houseworth-Weston, L. (2018). Breaking barriers: why Black-owned beauty stores are important and on the rise. Essence, Essence Magazine. Retrieved August 4, 2019, from www.essence.com/beauty/black-owned-beauty-supply-stores-important/.

Johnson, K. (2018, November 14). *Former waitress, now natural hair entrepreneur, shares lessons learned.* Black Enterprise. Retrieved July 29, 2019, from www.blackenterprise.com/lessons-natural-hair-entrepreneur/

Mintel. (2018). *Natural hair movement drives sales of styling products in US black haircare market.* Beauty and Personal Care, Mintel. Retrieved July 29, 2019, from http://www.mintel.com/press-centre/beauty-and-personal-care/natural-hair-movement-drives-sales-of-styling-products-in-us-black-haircare-market

Mintel. (2017). *Black haircare regimens boost shampoo sales in the US to reach $473 million in 2017.* Beauty and Personal Care, Mintel. Retrieved July 29, 2019, http://www.mintel.com/press-centre/beauty-and-personal-care/black-haircare-regimens-boost-shampoo-sales-in-the-us

Okoroafor, C. (2017, October 3). Inspiringly eclectic hairstyles and their origins across Africa." Culture Trip, The

References

Culture Trip. Retrieved January 6, 2020, from https://theculturetrip.com/africa/nigeria/articles/inspiring-hairstyles-and-their-origins-across-africa/

Opiah, A. (2014, 25 March). The changing business of Black hair, a potentially $500B industry. HuffPost. Retrieved March 30, 2014, from www.huffpost.com/entry/the-changing-business-of_b_4650819

Shatzman, C. (2018, December 28). Miss Rizos on how to wear your hair natural and changing the way we think about curls. Forbes. Retrieved February 7, 2020, from https://www.forbes.com/sites/celiashatzman/2018/12/28/miss-rizos-on-how-to-wear-your-hair-natural-and-changing-the-way-we-think-about-curls/#5613d7207d26

References Chapter 3

Antonia. (2019, May 15). Crochet braids, everything you need to know. Unruly. Retrieved January 15, 2020, from un-ruly.com/crochet-braids-everything-you-need-to-know/.

Asea Mae. (2019, March 8). *LCO vs LOC method on natural*

hair: which method is better for 4c hair? AseaMea Beauty. Retrieved January 28, 2020, from https://aseamaebeauty.com/blog/lco-vs-loc-method

Ashe, B. (2015). Agate Bolden.

Bey, J. (2011, June 8). *'Going natural' requires lots of help.* The New York Times. Retrieved April 19, 2014, from http://www.nytimes.com/2011/06/09/fashion/hair-care-for-african-americans.html?_r=1&2014

Black Girl Long Hair. (2015, May 24). *14 Photos of Ethiopian Tribespeople Who Use Butter to Style Their Hair.* Black Girl Long Hair. Retrieved March 25, 2020, from https://bglh-marketplace.com/2015/05/ethiopian-tribes-use-butter-to-style-natural-hair/

Ellington, T. N. (2014). Social networking sites: a support system for African-American women wearing natural hair. International Journal of Fashion Design, Technology and Education, 4 (9), 552-564.

Gabbara, P. (2016). The history of dreadlocks. Ebony Magazine. Retrieved March 25, 2020, from https://www.ebony.com/style/history-dreadlocks/

References

Goswami, S., Köbler, F., Leimeister, J. M., & Kremar, H. (2010). Using online social networking to enhance social connectedness and social support for the elderly. *Proceedings of International Conference on Information Systems (ICIS) 2010*. St. Louis, MO.

Holy Bible. Judges 13-16. New Living Translation. Tyndale House Foundation. Tyndale House Publisher, 1996, 2004, 2007, 2015.

Holy Bible. Revelations 5:5. New Living Translation. Tyndale House Foundation. Tyndale House Publisher, 1996, 2004, 2007, 2015.

Keating, D. M. (2013). Spirituality and support: A descriptive analysis of online social support for depression. *Journal of Religion and Health, 52* (3), 1014-1028.

Kira. (n.d.) Dreadlocks: the only guide you'll ever need. Curl Centric. Retrieved March 25, 2020, from https://www.curlcentric.com/dreadlocks/#the_stages_of_dreadlocks

Knight, H. About the founder. ILoveMyFro. Retrieved January 28, 2020, from https://www.ilovemyfro.com/about

Knight, H (ILoveMyFro). *Oils are not moisturizers* [Video].

YouTube. Retrieved January 28, 2020, from https://www.youtube.com/watch?v=D33ZIWIR4q0

Kroubo Dagnini, J. (2009). Rastafari: alternative religion and resistance against "white" Christianit. Études caribéennes [En ligne]. https://doi.org/10.4000/etudescaribeennes.3665

Meyerson, C. (2019, June 18). *The YouTubers who changed the landscape for #NaturalHair*. Wired, Conde Nast. Retrieved January 15, 2020, from www.wired.com/story/youtube-natural-hair/

Moore, C. (2019, October 2). What Is the LOC Method? Here's Everything You Should Know.Byrdie.com. Retrieved January 28, 2020, from https://www.byrdie.com/the-loc-method-4771726

Opiah, A. (2014, March 25). *The changing business of Black hair, potentially $500B industry*. HuffPost. Retrieved March 20, 2014, from www.huffpost.com/entry/the-changing-business-of_b_4650819

References

References Chapter 4

Achebe, C. (2014, July 29). *Are you a natural hair Nazi?* BlackDoctor, BlackDoctor Inc. Retrieved May 16, 2020 from https://blackdoctor.org/natural-hair-nazis/

Achenbach, J. (2009, May 1). Study finds Africans more genetically diverse than other populations. The Washington Post, WP Company. Retrieved May 4, 2010, from www.washingtonpost.com/wp-dyn/content/article/2009/04/30/AR2009043002485.html

A'Cylo. (2019, February 18). *Texturism: An Underlying Layer to Colorism.* DDS Magazine. Retrieved April 18, 2019, from https://www.ddsmagazine.com/single-post/2019/02/17/Texturism-An-Underlying-Layer-to-Colorism

African Export (AFRICANEXPORT). (2014, February 26). *Natural hair: my favorite styler, products that work for me (dry, coarse, high porosity)* [Video]. YouTube. Retrieved May 16, 2020, from https://youtu.be/jBrEfvM8IC0

American Academy of Dermatology. (n.d.). *Are your hair care products causing breakouts?* American Academy of Dermatology Association. Retrieved May 16, 2020, from www.aad.org/public/diseases/acne/causes/hair-products

ChemicalSafetyFacts.org. (n.d.) Mineral Oil. Chemical Safety Facts. Retrieved May 16, 2020, from www.chemicalsafetyfacts.org/mineral-oil/.

Cornwell, P. A. (2017). A review of shampoo surfactant technology: consumer benefits, raw materials and recent developments. *International Journal of Cosmetic Science, 40* (1), 16-30. https://doi.org/10.1111/ics.12439

Efik, Z. (EfikZara). (2019, December 29). *5 big lies the natural hair community lied about grease!!* [Video]. YouTube. Retrieved May 16, 2020 from https://www.youtube.com/watch?v=EsUzlJAGQWA

Fulton, J. E. (2001). *Acne RX: what acne really is and how to eliminate its devastating effects!* Self-published.

Greaves, K. (2019, March 4). 4C hair influencers share how texture discrimination within the Black community affects them on social media." Bustle. Retrieved April

References

28, 2020, from

https://www.bustle.com/p/4c-hair-influencers-share-how-texture-discrimination-within-the-black-community-affects-them-on-social-media-16243800

Harrell, Y. (2015). *The development of microaggressions in the online natural hair community: a thematic analysis* (Publication No. 27). [Master thesis, Georgia State University]. ScholarWorks at GSU, https://scholarworks.gsu.edu/aas_theses/27

Hernandez, N. (2018, April 8). FEATURISM: IS VERY REAL. Medium. Retrieved April 18, 2020, from https://medium.com/@lamentedlania/featurism-is-very-real-23d32d425d1e

Hope, I. (2018, December 5). *Natural hair police | why people hate the natural hair community | rant* [Video]. YouTube. Retrieved May 11, 2020, from https://www.youtube.com/watch?v=jJ4Je9u22-8

Japour, M. J. (1939). *Petroleum Refining and Manufacturing Processes.* Wetzel Publishing Company, Inc.

Joynavon (JOYNAVON). (2016, June 27). *Flat twist out on*

short 4C natural hair [Video]. YouTube. Retrieved May 5, 2020, from https://www.youtube.com/watch?v=S4P5M_-2z_I

Joynavon (JOYNAVON). (2019, August 20). *Y'all don't give a d**n about short 4c natural hair! Period* [Video]. YouTube. Retrieved May 5, 2020, from https://www.youtube.com/watch?v=Bt4T-T3zR_0&t=1207s

Kilahmazing. (2019, June 14). *4C hair isn't appreciated until it's long* [Video]. YouTube. Retrieved May 5, 2020, from https://www.youtube.com/watch?v=CzYpqgK_mz0

Lin, A., Nabatian, A., & C. P. Halverstam. (2017). Discovering black soap: a survey on the attitudes and practices of black soap users." The journal of clinical and aesthetic dermatology 10 (7), 18-22. PMID: 29104719

Reece, R. L. (2018). Genesis of U.S. Colorism and skin tone stratification: slavery, freedom, and mulatto-Black occupational inequality in the late 19th century. *The Review of Black Political Economy, 45* (1), 3–21.

References

https://doi.org/10.1177/0034644618770761

Sethi, A., Kaur, T., Malhotra, S.K., & M.L. Gambhir. (2016). Moisturizers: the slippery road. *Indian journal of dermatology 61*, (3), 279-87. https://doi.org/10.4103/0019-5154.182427

Turgeon, A. & E. Morse. (2018). Petroleum. 14 Jan. 2013. National Geographic Society. Retrieved 16, May 2020, www.nationalgeographic.org/encyclopedia/petroleum/

Yvonne, K. (2017, January 23). *I hate the natural hair community + natural hair Nazis* [Video]. YouTube. Retrieved May 8, 2020, from https://www.youtube.com/watch?v=1XwjKzdo7KQ

References Chapter 5

Bryant, T. (2015, May 29). *Why calling this hairstyle 'twisted mini-buns' is offensive*. Refinery29, Vice Media Group. Retrieved June 10, 2020, from www.refinery29.com/en-us/2015/05/88254/bantu-knots-cultural-appropriation

Culturally Situated Design Tools (CSDT). (n.d.) *African Origins of Cornrows*. African Origins. CSDT. Retrieved

June 10, June 2020, from https://csdt.org/culture/cornrowcurves/origins.html

Grays, J. (2016). *The Blurred Lines of Cultural Appropriation* (Publication No. 181). [Master thesis, CUNY Graduate School of Journalism], 2016. CUNY Academic Works. Retrieved June 10, 2020, from https://academicworks.cuny.edu/gj_etds/181/

Hairunruled. (2018, April 16). Can white women be in the natural hair movement? | Black Hair Is... [Video]. YouTube. Retrieved May 21, 2020, from

https://www.youtube.com/watch?v=baNZauyRnLs

Horne, M. (2018, February 28). *A visual history of iconic Black hairstyles*. History.com, A&E Television Networks. Retrieved June 10,2020, from www.history.com/news/black-hairstyles-visual-history-in-photos

pound_cake [@KiaSpeaks]. (2017, April 24). *I really don't get why y'all are mad at Shea Moisture. Y'all should want black businesses to start getting this white coin as well* [Tweet]. Twitter. https://twitter.com/KiaSpeaks/sta-

References

tus/856573413237940226

1BlessedNatural. (2013, September 9). *Asian Hair Trend: Afro Perms*. Blogger, Retrieved June 10, 2020 from www.1blessednatural.com/2013/09/asian-hair-trend-afro-perms.html

Opiah, A. (2018, May 19). *What is Black hair?* Un-Ruly. Retrieved May 21, 2020, from https://un-ruly.com/what-is-black-hair/

Payne, A. & Duster, C. R.. (2017, April 25). *Shea Moisture ad falls flat under backlash. Ad Falls Flat Under Backlash*. NBCNews.com, NBCUniversal News Group. Retrieved May 18, 2020, from www.nbcnews.com/news/nbcblk/shea-moisture-ad-falls-flat-after-backlash-n750421

Mullen, R. (n.d.). *About Me*. RoryMullen.com. Retrieved May 25, 2020, from www.rorymullen.com/p/about.html.

Safronova, V. (2016, September 16). *Marc Jacobs's use of faux locs on models draws social media ire*. The New York Times. Retrieved June 10, 2020, from www.nytimes.com/2016/09/18/fashion/marc-jacobs-models-dreadlocks-social-media-response-new-york-fashion-week.html.

Swint, T. (n.d.). *About the Organization.* Styles4Kidz, Styles 4 Kidz NFP. Retrieved June 10, 2020, from www.styles4kidz.org/about

Tharps, L. (2018, November 28). Asian men getting afros: it's officially a thing! *MyAmericanMeltingpot.* Retrieved June 10, 2020, from www.myamericanmeltingpot.com/2018/11/28/asian-men-afros-trend/

Trudy [@thetrudz]. (2017, April 24). *Shea Moisture been drew a line in the sand, but now they're throwing the sand in the eyes of dark BW (Black Women) w/ kinky hair* [Tweet]. Twitter. https://twitter.com/thetrudz/status/856578223966171137?lang=en

Varma-White, K. (2014, April 8). *White Moms, Black Hair: Blogs Teach Adoptive and Interracial Families.* TODAY.com, NBC Universal. Retrieved May 25, 2020, from www.today.com/parents/white-moms-black-hair-blogs-teach-adoptive-interracial-families-care-2D79488068.

References

References Chapter 6

Asmelash, L. (2020, January 24). *If This Texas Student Doesn't Cut His Dreadlocks, He Won't Get to Walk at Graduation. It's Another Example of Hair Discrimination, Some Say*. CNN. Retrieved June 21, 2020, from www.cnn.com/2020/01/23/us/barbers-hill-isd-dreadlocks-deandre-arnold-trnd/index.html.

Bowser, Y. L. (Creator). (1993-1998). *Living single* [TV series]. Fox Broadcasting Company.

Bowser, Y.L, & D. Wyatt. (Writers). (1994). A Hair-Razing Experience (Season 2, Episode 13) [TV series episode]. In Y.L. Bowser (creator), *Living Single,* Fox Broadcasting Company.

CROWN Act. *The Official Campaign of The CROWN ACT 2019*. The CROWN Collective. Retrieved June 21, 2020, from www.thecrownact.com/

Diaz, T. (2020, February 9). DeAndre Arnold proudly wears his locs to the Oscars after being banned from graduation." Refinery29, Vice Group. Retrieved June 21, 2020, from www.refinery29.com/en-us/2020/02/9383456/deandre-arnold-oscars-dreadlocks-hair-love-2020.

Griffin, C. (2019, July 3). *How natural black hair at work became a civil rights issue.* JSTOR Daily, JSTOR. Retrieved June 16, 2020 from https://daily.jstor.org/how-natural-black-hair-at-work-became-a-civil-rights-issue

Ibram X. Kendi [@DrIbram]. (2020, Jan. 23). *By demanding a student cut his locs, your expectations are actually quite low for your students. There's nothing lower than teaching students to not respect cultural difference. There's nothing lower than teaching students cultural racism* [Tweet]. https://twitter.com/DrIbram/status/1220492414634414080

Be A King [@BerniceKing]. (2020, January 22). *"Deandre's locs do not reflect "lowness" or a deviation from what should be a "high expectation" at a school trying to reflect the Beloved Community* [Tweet]. Twitter. https://twitter.com/BerniceKing/status/1220197041076428803

Murphy, R., & A. Daniel. (2019, April 5). School Districts. Texas Public Schools. Retrieved June 21, 2020, from

References

https://schools.texastribune.org/districts/

State of New Jersey. (2010, December 19). *Governor Murphy Signs Legislation Clarifying That Discrimination Based on Hairstyles Associated with Race Is Illegal.* Official Site of the State of New Jersey. Retrieved June 21, 2020, from www.nj.gov/governor/news/news/562019/20191219c.shtml

New York State. (2019, July 2016). Governor Cuomo signs S6209A/A7797A to make clear civil rights law bans discrimination against hair styles or textures associated with race. To Make Clear Civil Rights Laws Ban Discrimination Against Hair Styles Or Textures Associated With Race." Governor.ny.gov. Retrieved June 21, 2020, from www.governor.ny.gov/news/governor-cuomo-signs-s6209aa7797a-make-clear-civil-rights-laws-ban-discrimination-against-hair

Beverly Jeanne Jenkins, v. Blue Cross Mutual Hospital Insurance, Inc., and Blue Shield Mutual Medical Insurance, Inc538 F.2d 164. . Retrieved June 18, 2020, from https://openjurist.org/538/f2d/164/jenkins-v-blue-cross-mutual-hospital-insurance-inc#fn1

Wamsley, L. (2018, December 27). Adults Come Under Scrutiny After HS Wrestler Told To Cut His Dreadlocks Or Forfeit. Race, NPR. Retrieved June 21, 2020, www.npr.org/2018/12/27/680470933/after-h-s-wrestler-told-to-cut-his-dreadlocks-or-forfeit-adults-come-under-scrut.

References Chapter 7

Ashanti. (2014, March 10). *Ashanti Interview at Breakfast Club Power 105 1 (March 2014)* [Video]. YouTube. Retrieved July 27, 2020, from https://youtu.be/jh-gv38kiBUU

References

UNRAVELING THE STORY OF BLACK/AFRICAN HAIR

www.ingramcontent.com/pod-product-compliance
Lightning Source LLC
Chambersburg PA
CBHW071429070526
44578CB00001B/49